T0330380

Tourism as a Form of International Relations

Στον Κυριάκο και τον Αντώνη

Tourism as a Form of International Relations

Insights from Contemporary Practice

Katerina Antoniou

Lecturer, School of Business and Management, University of Central Lancashire, Cyprus

Edward Elgar
PUBLISHING

Cheltenham, UK • Northampton, MA, USA

Published by
Edward Elgar Publishing Limited
The Lypiatts
15 Lansdown Road
Cheltenham
Glos GL50 2JA
UK

Edward Elgar Publishing, Inc.
William Pratt House
9 Dewey Court
Northampton
Massachusetts 01060
USA

A catalogue record for this book
is available from the British Library

Library of Congress Control Number: 2023939692

This book is available electronically in the **Elgar**online
Geography, Planning and Tourism subject collection
http://dx.doi.org/10.4337/9781802207774

ISBN 978 1 80220 776 7 (cased)
ISBN 978 1 80220 777 4 (eBook)

Printed and bound in Great Britain by
TJ Books Limited, Padstow, Cornwall

Contents

Figures

Tables

Acknowledgements

To Anna and Michael, thank you for guiding me through this interdisciplinary journey.

To Stelios, thank you for always having my back.

Abbreviations

AU	African Union
EU	European Union
G7	Group of 7
G20	Group of 20
GPI	Global Peace Index
IEP	Institute for Economics and Peace
IR	International Relations
MICE	Meetings, Incentives, Conferences and Exhibitions
NATO	North Atlantic Treaty Organisation
P2P Accommodation	Peer-to-Peer Accommodation
PPR	Positive Peace Report
R2P	Responsibility to Protect
RSCT	Regional Security Complex Theory
SCORE	Social Cohesion and Reconciliation Index
SDGs	Sustainable Development Goals
SeeD	Centre for Sustainable Peace and Democratic Development
UK	United Kingdom
UN	United Nations
UNDP	United Nations Development Programme
UNDP-ACT	United Nations Development Programme – Action for Cooperation and Trust in Cyprus
UNEP	United Nations Environment Programme
US	United States
VFR	visiting friends and relatives

Tourism as a Form of International Relations: an introduction

In February 2022, the Russian army performed a military intervention in Ukraine, resulting in numerous fatalities, infrastructural damage, and millions of Ukrainians forcibly displaced from their homes. What has thereafter been referred to as the 2022 Russia–Ukraine war is underway for over a year without a peace settlement in sight. In response to Russia's offensive military action against its sovereign neighbour, Western alliances and individual states have aligned with Ukraine on a political, military, and social level and responded with sanctions and criticism to the Russian government, led by President Vladimir Putin. One of the responses to Russia's military intervention was a range of sanctions from the European Union targeting the Russian government, its businesses, and individual citizens, with one measure being the decision on increased visa restrictions for Russian citizens travelling to the European Union (Turner, 2022).

The Russia–Ukraine war is undoubtedly a catalytic event in contemporary international relations. It is a benchmark in the discourse of contemporary international affairs, one that directly involves state actors, but at the same time affects supranational and non-governmental entities, civil society, and individual citizens. Petr Lovigin, a Russian travel vlogger with more than half a million followers, and Leanid Pashkouski, a Belarusian travel vlogger with over one million followers, suggest that international political decisions aimed at states do not only affect the state actors targeted, but also their citizens, who should be treated as separate non-state actors with the capacity to influence global affairs in a direction different from their affiliated state.

> [EU] sanctions [against Russia] target those [Russians that are] against the war. [...] this is completely unfair because at least among young Russians, I've hardly met anyone who supports the war. The European Union thereby makes life as difficult as possible for those who are trying to fight the regime. It won't help. I still do not see a single sanction from the West that would stop this war and Putin's actions. (Petr Lovigin, Russian Travel Vlogger; Turner, 2022)

> [The EU] often equates Russia and Belarus. I think these restrictions are just senseless, ineffective moves made by the EU authorities instead of doing real things. In reality it won't stop Putin, it won't help to win the war, it won't even prevent the Russians from travelling. Instead, such sanctions could definitely have an opposite

effect: people in Russia will consolidate more and more around Putin's ideology – because they see the whole world hating and cancelling them. Those who have the possibility to travel are in opposition to the regime most of the time, so the EU is hitting its allies. (Leanid Pashkouski, Belarusian Travel Vlogger; Turner, 2022)

The statements made by Lovigin and Pashkouski explain that a state-centric political response does not effectively encapsulate the diversity of state and non-state actors involved in contemporary international relations and in conflict more specifically. The assumption that states are unitary bodies overlooks the impact of their citizens as separate political actors, an impact often generated – as these vloggers suggest – through the act of travel.

Contemporary international relations call for a reconceptualization of who is a political actor and who is affected by international political discourse. Did the EU falsely respond to the war in a state-centric approach? Do individual citizens have the capacity to shape global affairs and, if so, in what ways? Does tourism and international travel have a role to play in shaping international relations and in engaging unconventional political actors such as citizens? This book is set to examine these questions and discuss international affairs, contemporary global phenomena, and international tourism dynamics to identify the impact of tourists as emerging political actors. Through the deconstruction of conventional international relations, this book is set to reconceptualize tourism as a form of international relations.

TOURISM THROUGH THE IR LENS

Scholarship has defined tourism as the temporary visitation of people to destinations and therefore much of this scholarship has focused on exploring the relationship between people and places. Admittedly, this is a central component of tourism. Nevertheless, tourism is also the exchange of information across people. It is an activity that allows people to become transmitters of knowledge and emotions, agents of intercultural dialogue, illustrators of social norms from across the globe. Conceptualizing tourism in its broader capacity as a people-to-people exchange reveals the bigger picture of tourist activity and its impact beyond the conventional focus on tourism as an activity of leisure and recreation. Seeing tourism as a transnational practice with political, economic, social, and ethical repercussions allows tourism to be redefined beyond individual travel preferences and motivations. It goes beyond the person and what they do for recreation, and it goes well beyond the relationship between people and places. Today tourism is a form of transnational networking enabling the exchange of information across individuals and communities. Tourism has become, to a great extent, about the relationships formed and exchanges made between people; and the socio-political impacts arising from these relations and interactions today lie at the forefront of tourism research. In other words, the study of tourism has evolved enough to deviate from a destination-centric starting point to become more focused on people-to-people socio-political interaction. The study of tourism as an international activity is, therefore, a component of international studies.

To reconceptualize tourism from this perspective, paying attention to the socio-political impacts it generates, introduces tourism as a novel and yet basic form of international relations. The study of tourism as a socio-political activity within the scope of international studies places tourism at the heart of International Relations, or IR. An interdisciplinary field within the Political Sciences, studies of International Relations examine international socio-political activity, and although its engagement with tourism has thus far been limited, there is a direct connection between contemporary international affairs and tourism as a contemporary socio-political phenomenon that can be incorporated within the IR field of study.

International Relations has been conventionally about the study of interstate relations, treating states as the principal political actors of the world stage. Through a continuously evolving scholarly discourse, IR today is no longer about the relations between states, and to an analogous extent the study of tourism is no longer confined to examining the interaction between people and destinations within the realm of leisure and escapism. The field of International Relations has become concerned with political agents, institutional entities, organization representatives, and individuals, interacting on a transnational scale. It thus entails the interaction between people from other cultures and other communities, and tourism engages with exactly that. In its contemporary form, tourism conducts international relations in the modern era. It is for this reason that understanding Tourism as a form of International Relations is crucial for the evolution and advancement of both fields.

Tourism has evolved as an academic field that is not only informed by, but also informs conflict resolution, foreign affairs, media, communication, geography, and social psychology. Tourism has evolved to become central to the very exchange of socio-political information, an exchange that was interrupted during the 2020 COVID-19 pandemic and, as a result, the effortless, interpersonal exchange of information, cultures, concepts, and trends was also halted. As tourism revives in a post-pandemic era, we have the responsibility to examine it beyond its conventional, destination-centric version; a version that is outdated. Tourism is not simply the activity of holidaymaking and vacationing. Tourism is about shaping the world dynamically, organically, and constantly.

Rourke and Boyer (2008) insightfully reference Shakespeare's words that "the world is a stage and all the men and women merely players" to highlight the scope of international relations, and to emphasize the range of characters, incentives and dynamics involved in world politics. Besides examining the actors involved on the international political stage, the field of International Relations reviews the structures and conditions through which these actors interact. These structures, perspectives and overall ontological standpoints of IR provide the lens(es) through which tourism can be revisited. This book uses theories, conceptual frameworks, methodologies, and levels of analysis employed within the IR field to discuss contemporary tourist activity, and accordingly, view tourism through the IR lens.

Why IR as a Lens?

International Relations is a field that has been intricately linked with Political Sciences and has been defined as the examination of political activity on an international scale across state and non-state actors. States have been conventionally considered the primary actors of the international political stage, and as such the actors that shape international politics. The emergence of global phenomena, the ever-increasing interconnectedness and interdependence of international political actors, and the undertaking of international activity from a plethora of both state and non-state actors has reshaped the field dramatically in the modern era. Today, the field of IR does not automatically imply inter-state relations and dynamics. That is simply a component of the discipline that has been studied "the longest" (Aydınlı and Biltekin, 2018).

What is undoubtedly a commonality between Tourism and IR is their inherently interdisciplinary nature. Tourism research informs and is informed by various academic disciplines, with the field illustrating an interconnectedness to social science disciplines such as Sociology, Anthropology, Economic Sciences, Business and Management, Social Psychology and Geography. In an analogous manner, IR and its emergence as a distinct academic field was characterized by a frequent exchange of scholarly ideas with other fields, primarily the ones informing Tourism as well. According to Aydınlı and Biltekin (2018), IR scholarship has widened in scope and has become more sophisticated over the decades by welcoming input from other disciplines. To draw distinct boundaries between disciplines of the social sciences is futile, as each discipline provides a distinct perspective through which socio-political activities, interactions and phenomena can be examined. If more work within the social sciences is conducted in an interdisciplinary manner, scholars will acknowledge the benefits that come with the interconnectedness of these fields, and will more comprehensively understand the socio-political activities, interactions, and phenomena these disciplines examine.

A question worth asking is why is tourism not already incorporated within the scholarly spectrum of International Relations? A discipline examining intercultural exchanges with evident socio-political impact is oddly marginalized from the study of international political discourse. This is primarily because IR has traditionally focused on states as the principal political actors and has only recently revisited its scope to include non-state actors. Tourism is still considered a predominantly socioeconomic activity and remains disconnected from international political affairs. This book seeks to contest this discrepancy by introducing the ways in which the tourist holds the capacity to perform political acts and shape international affairs.

One of the criticisms received by the field of International Relations in recent decades is that it has failed to explain and predict emerging trends and phenomena on the world stage. Widening the IR scope and revisiting the actors engaging in international political affairs is not only an approach that reveals the political contributions of tourism, but a scholarly innovation that will assist the IR field to escape its conceptual stalemate and engage with the study of international affairs more comprehensively. In bridging the gap between Tourism and IR, this book introduces Tourism as a form of International Relations and examines the magnitude and implications of its socio-political impact through the lens of IR theories, and levels of analysis.

The IR field offers three levels of analysis, or three perspectives with a separate focus to identify, explain, and evaluate political activity in the international stage. These are namely (1) the individual/organizational level, (2) the state level, which has been a dominant level of analysis in the field, and (3) the systemic level. When considering the three levels of analysis in reference to the study of non-state political actors, the systemic level has been considered as the most applicable to their examination, due to the approach's attention to global dynamics and phenomena. For examining the tourist as a non-state political actor, the individual level of analysis becomes an insightful tool that can attend to personal motivations and individual political acts that mount up to inform global movements. The three levels are more extensively examined in Chapter 1, as an analytical approach to understanding the role of tourism in contemporary diplomacy.

TOURISM AS AN EVOLVING INTERNATIONAL PRACTICE

A key reference for discussing the evolution of modern tourism is the twentieth century's Fordism period. The era of Fordism developed following the Industrial Revolution and was identified as the era of mass production (Amin, 1994). Despite its reference to the economic structures of the twentieth century, Fordism has also referred to other parameters of society, such as culture and social change, and has been linked to individual behaviour, such as consumerism and travelling, as well as collective identity (Hall, 1988).

The 1970s saw a new trend in tourism that emerged in the United States, and it was the development of tourist environmental bubbles. Stors and Kagermeier (2013) define tourist bubbles as tourist-designated infrastructure separated from the city and isolated from what were considered as unhospitable and threatening urban environments. Tourist bubbles were designed as "leisure and entertainment districts" (2013: 117), with the purpose of providing safety to the visitors. Ironically, tourist bubbles enabled visitors to access new destinations without coming into direct contact with them.

The twentieth century was not only characterized by Fordism's industrial revolution paving the way for mass production and consumption, it was also defined by a bipolar political system of two superpowers – the United States and the Soviet Union – and the ideological warfare they engaged in during the Cold War. The end of the Cold War saw the collapse of the Soviet Union and the reshaping of the world stage with the US as the acting global hegemon. A prominent approach for describing the international scene during the late twentieth century and specifically within the post-Cold War era is the distinction between Western vs other political actors. Stemming not only from economic performance, but also from socio-political, ideological, and geographical parameters, the "West vs the rest" classification acknowledges how Western political ideology and socioeconomic activity overwhelmingly spread across the globe in the post-Cold War era of US political hegemony. A Western culture of mass consumerism, and what was critiqued as West's aggressive economic imperialism, was characterized by resource exploitation, unfair economic interactions, and political domination (Petras, 1994; Kapur, 1997; Easterly, 2002; Friedman, 2005). The phenomenon that was characterized as Westernization was interlinked with the process of globalization, or the ability of states and actors across the globe to become closely interconnected. Technological growth, transnational trade, political stability, and financially viable travel options made the world come closer together, as if it were "flat" (Friedman, 2005).

Like other US-based trends, the tourist environmental bubble phenomenon spread widely on a global scale soon after the amplification of globalization in the late 1990s. When tourist bubbles grew into a global phenomenon, they featured standardized amenities and utilities, often through known western brands, hotel chains, and restaurant/cafe franchises. They therefore provided not only a safe zone for visitors, but also a westernized area in each destination. Touristification, or the process through which segments of urban settings developed into "complete tourist zones" (Stors and Kagermeier, 2013: 118), became a process of destination Westernization. International tourist bubbles offered western tourist infrastructure across the world, including known fast food and coffeeshop chains and created a sense of comfort through recognizable providers and expected quality of service. They endorsed a type of tourism that was more convenient and superficial and less engaging with local attitudes and trends.

During the 1980s and 1990s, scholarship spoke of the end of the Fordist era, substituted by a post-Fordist organizational model, characterized by new forms of economic and political governance that deviated from the mass production model. Amin (1994) identifies three approaches to the transition from Fordism to post-Fordism – or neo-Fordism – which can be seen as contemporary mechanisms of economic governance. The regulatory approach speaks of a norm that started in the 1970s in France and attempted to establish institutional regulations over the capitalist economic model to provide increased economic stability and prolonged growth. The second approach is defined as the neo-Schumpeterian and shares aspirations analogous to the regulatory approach, including the aim to prolong the cycle of economic growth, with the difference in the latter's emphasis on technology and technical standards (ibid.). The third approach, flexible specialization, deviates from mass production through unskilled labour by endorsing skilled, specialized labour of customized goods (Piore and Sabel, 1984; Amin, 1994). According to Hirst and Zeitlin (1991), the flexible specialization approach acknowledges multiple connections between institutions, politics, and technology.

The progression experienced by industrial discourse over the twentieth century, evolving from Fordism to post-Fordism was also mirrored by tourism discourse. International travel assumed, during the Fordist period, a character of mass consumption of the tourist product through mass tourism, travel packages organized in bulk, and trends of generic – and often superficial – interactions with a travel destination. This trend resulted in large inflows of tourism to designated destinations that featured adequate infrastructure to accommodate mass inflows of visitors, primarily engaging in seasonal vacationing and causing the phenomenon of seasonality in tourism. The economic trends of specialization, differentiation, and market segmentation that followed during the post-Fordism era were echoed by the tourist industry and paved the way for alternative forms of tourism to arise. These forms of tourism differentiated in the types of activities they incorporated and were often delivered in smaller groups – or at an individual traveller's level – making tourist experiences more customized and spreading tourist activity more widely across available destinations and throughout seasons. Today, the tourism scene is characterized by an ever-growing variety of options for both organized mass travel and customized individual experiences, making the diversity of tourist activity wider than ever before.

In the early 1990s, at the dawn of the globalization phenomenon and considering the shift towards a post-Cold War era, Huntington developed what is considered a fundamental text for the systemic analysis of global world order, the Clash of Civilizations. Huntington's (1993) account, following the demand of the 1990s, attempted to address the shift from a bi-polar Cold War international system to a new era, and predicted that the main source of conflict would be ideological and would occur between the major civilizations of the world. These included the Western, the Latin American, the Orthodox, the Eastern, the Muslim, and the Sub-Saharan. Huntington's approach was contradicted by literature that spoke of a unipolar world having emerged from the end of the Cold War, with the US acting as a global hegemon (Heisbourg, 1999; Cameron, 2002), while a third perspective replaced the US hegemony rhetoric with a multipolar international system of multiple global powers and emerging new hegemons (Buzan and Wæver, 2003; Colin et al., 2007; Lennon and Kozlowski, 2008; Bulmer and Paterson, 2013).

In the decades that followed and led up to the 2020 Coronavirus pandemic, the field of International Relations witnessed the emergence of non-state political actors. While international affairs were dominated by the discussions on terrorism as a transnational, non-state threat to state sovereignty, additional non-state political influencers of the world stage were also introduced, including global movements and global civil society (Kaldor, 2003, 2020; Keane, 2003). Kaldor (2020) highlights that civil society is a consensual form of citizen participation in international politics, it has transnational impact, and can directly inform global governance and international security. Global civil society movements are directly interlinked with voluntary, short-term mobility across state borders, and hence hold a direct connection to patterns of international tourist activity.

From terrorism to economic and environmental crises, to a pandemic, the world witnessed many threats occurring at an international scale, and as such security responses have also moved beyond national fronts to multiple forms of international security. Buzan et al. (1998) presented five sectors for the effective analysis of contemporary international security within the framework of the Copenhagen School of Security Studies. The sectors of security identified are military, environmental, economic, societal, and political and they each entail the capacity of receiving existential threats articulated and constructed by a securitizing agent. The Copenhagen School effectively introduced the socially constructed nature of international security with succeeding securitization scholarship indicating that threats can be both constructed and deconstructed by political actors (Butler, 2020). The contribution of tourism to processes of securitization, desecuritization, and international security is identified and discussed subsequently in this book with direct reference to Buzan et al.'s five sectors of international security.

Understanding tourism as a form of international relations requires placing Tourism within the IR theoretical framework, and in doing that effectively it is vital to understand the dominant IR theories as separate viewpoints within the field, each providing its distinct set of assumptions and expectations regarding international political activity. Some IR theoretical frameworks are more state-centric, others attend to individual capacities, and some put an emphasis on the international stage and its ability to engage multiple actors. State-centric theories assume the unchanging dominance of state actors and the static nature of their goals and encounters, making them less effective in capturing the emergence of new political actors with a differentiated approach to international relations. The following section reviews key IR theories and their ability to understand tourism as a contemporary form of international political activity.

THEORIES OF INTERNATIONAL RELATIONS AND TOURISM

The Realist school of thought was one of the initial theoretical frameworks developed for understanding international relations (Rourke and Boyer, 2008; Burchill et al., 2009). Niccolo Machiavelli and Thomas Hobbes are the early theorists of Realism, while prominent figures of the twentieth century include Morgenthau, Waltz, Carr, Mearsheimer, Niebuhr, and Kennan (Donnelly, 2009). Realism focuses on the constraints of international politics imposed by inherent human egoism, acting in the absence of an international world system and instead operating within the Westphalian system of state anarchy (ibid.). Realism understands the interaction across political actors as the inevitable egoistic quest for survival, one that will inevitably lead to antagonism and conflict.

The theory of Neorealism, which emerged through basic principles of realism, distinguishes the behaviouralist attributes of old realism from Neorealism's attention to structure. While old realism explains international relations through state behaviour and decision-making, Neorealism puts this behavioural approach in context by identifying the structural framework that restricts or enables state behaviour (Waltz, 2004).

Realism is viewed as one of the two primary theoretical frameworks that have defined the IR field's course of evolution. The second of the two is Liberalism. Liberal scholars, including Rousseau, Kant, Schumpeter, and Doyle, argue that peace, not war, is the natural state of being (Burchill, 2009). Kant's 1975 account on Perpetual Peace has been an emblematic account for the theory of Liberalism, which emphasizes human ability to operate under win–win situations and to seek cooperation and interdependent prosperity.

The liberal model of cooperation placed an early emphasis on economic interdependence, which evolved to the notion of Neoliberalism, supporting free trade and emphasizing democratic values as a prerequisite for transnational cooperation. Neoliberalism advocates for increased collaboration among international political actors, acknowledging the notion of self-sufficient states as unrealistic (ibid.). Powell (1994) argues that both Neoliberalism and Neorealism face fundamental internal limitations that prevent them from contributing to the IR field in full magnitude.

When it comes to Realism, which looks at international relations as a zero-sum game, then looking at tourism from a realist perspective implies that tourism is to be considered as a zero-sum game activity within the realm of international relations. This perspective would emphasize the antagonistic relationship between host communities and visitor audiences: finite resources of destinations, space, infrastructure, and activities provided to tourists are perceived to be taken away from locals. In other words, the realist assumption poses the risk of heightening rival relations between the host and visitor populations in a particular destination. Additionally, government funds dispensed for supporting tourist structures and services could be perceived as taken away from attending to local needs. From a neorealist perspective, the tourist as a non-state actor would formulate their political contribution within the structures provided, which may hinder or prevent any tourist-driven political momentum from unfolding in an organic and unrestricted manner.

On the contrary, looking at tourism from a liberal perspective means that any form of tourist activity can be assumed as a solution from which everyone benefits. Through tourism, both tourists and local populations can benefit at the same time, considering that conditions are optimal for a win–win scenario to emerge. For example, infrastructures built for tourists are open to and accessible by locals. Enhancement of the arts and culture through the restoration of local architecture, the beautification of public spaces and the protection of heritage and archaeological sites is also of direct benefit to the host population. The economic and consumerist activity of tourists can support a wider range of shops and merchandise available to locals, while tourists also create higher demand for local events, exhibitions, and festivals, contributing to an improved standard of living and enhancing local well-being.

While Liberalism highlights the virtues of mutual benefits that could arise from international tourist activity, optimal conditions may not always be upheld, with discrepancies in host-visitor motivations, host-visitor expectations, and host-visitor cultural and ethical frameworks making win-win scenarios more complex to achieve. Both Realism and Liberalism present international affairs from opposite ends of a spectrum, with additional IR theories, such as the English School and Constructivism, seeking to bridge the gap between the two ends.

Constructivism and the English School are two theories that evolved subsequently to Realism and Liberalism and lie somewhere in the middle of the theoretical spectrum between the Realism and Liberalism extremes. From its commencement in the mid-twentieth century until today, the English School shows a direct connection to political theory, an aspect that strongly influences its methodological nature. Initially introduced by the British Committee during the 1950s, it focused primarily on the concept of international society. The Hedley Bull's (1977) Anarchical Society and Martin Wight's (1977) Systems of States developed as part of the English School's second phase and are considered foundational for the English School philosophy for further developing Western international society and placing the idea in historical context (ibid.).

Founding English School figures, such as Wight and Bull, developed their theoretical work in consideration of the normative debate between pluralism and solidarism, with subsequent English School literature developing under one of the two approaches (Buzan, 2004). The debate between pluralism and solidarism lies within international political theory and is concerned with the concept of international society. It refers, on the one hand, to the importance of the state as a sovereign institution within a diverse community of state actors and, on the other hand, to the respect of human rights within a cosmopolitan environment of universalism (Nardin, 2009). Pluralist rhetoric embraces the anarchical model to emphasize the heterogeneous coexistence of states under no formal superior authority, while solidarists reject this model of contemporary international society, calling for the necessity to institutionalize global order and international justice (ibid.).

In addition to the pluralist–solidarist distinction, English School thinkers can be identified according to their influences as realist, rationalist, or revolutionist. On one hand, the realist branch, including Hedley Bull and Robert Jackson, is directly influenced by Hobbesian realism, supporting that international society is more of a "social contract" rather than a natural, pre-defined condition (Wight in Buzan, 2004). On the other hand, revolutionist thinkers such as John Vincent, Nicholas Wheeler, and Timothy Dunne were inspired by Kantian idealism to endorse the idea of gradually transitioning from an international to a world society, further emphasizing the idea of progress and change within international relations. Consequently, revolutionists focus more on domestic politics, rejecting the idea of a society of states in aspiration of the world society of individuals (Buzan, 2004). It is accurate to assume that realist English School thinkers lie on the pluralist side of the theory's spectrum, while the revolutionists associate their views with the solidarist end of English School literature. With realist and revolutionist thinkers adopting contradictory arguments to one another, the rationalist position – adopted by Wight – comes to serve as the "via media" between the other two (Linklater, 2009: 97). Rationalist scholarship more accurately corresponds to the general philosophy of the English School as it rejects the utopianism of revolutionists and the real politik of realism, and at the same time provides the bridge between state-centric realist ideas and domestically focused revolutionists (ibid.: 88).

Constructivism, a theory that is close to the English School's philosophy, emerged long afterwards, at the end of the Cold War. In Guzzini's (2000: 147) words, Constructivism is "epistemologically about the social construction of knowledge and ontologically about the construction of social reality". The theory was soon welcomed as part of mainstream American IR (Reus-Smit, 2009). The end of the Cold War was an unexpected development within International Relations which rationalist mainstream IR theories, such as Neorealism and Neoliberalism, seemed incapable of explaining. The alternative to rationalist theories was critical theory, whose normative, non-empirical nature was often criticized as unsuitable to account for contemporary global politics. Consequently, Constructivism was soon welcomed as a middle-ground theoretical alternative: it was a non-rationalist perspective that was more empirical than critical theory (Rourke and Boyer, 2008; Reus-Smit, 2009).

Constructivist scholars are primarily divided into two streams: modernists and post-modernists. The post-modernist adopts a meta-theoretical approach with an emphasis on sociology and language to deconstruct basic structural assumptions and question accepted realities such as power, knowledge, sovereignty, and hierarchy (Bradley Phillips, 2007). Conversely, modern constructivists accept the existing social structures and provide an explanatory approach to international relations instead of a critique to the objectivity of "social truths" (Bradley Phillips, 2007: 64). The modernist approach is rejected by post-modernists as it affiliates with rationalist thinking and, hence, contradicts the non-rationalist nature of Constructivism that was a benchmark to its emergence. Post-modern constructivists, such as Martha Finnemore and Harald Müller, affiliate closely with post-structuralist ideas, such as the subjectivity of all knowledge, whereas modern constructivist figures such as Stephen Krasner and Alexander Wendt are more consistent with mainstream IR.

Alexander Wendt is a prominent constructivist scholar; his account of *Anarchy is What States Make of It* (1992) being considered a foundational text for Constructivism. Wendt contradicts the inevitability of human nature as portrayed by realism, and rationalism as embraced through Neoliberalism. More importantly, Wendt deconstructed the neorealist approach to anarchy, to argue that anarchical structures are not inherently constraining, but instead have been constructed through institutions that reflect social processes. Wendt's emphasis on structure evolved independently from other constructivist literature, gradually forming one of three theoretical branches, systemic constructivism. Until today, Wendt remains the most prominent supporter of systemic constructivism, emphasizing the importance of normative – or ideational – structures within international relations (Reus-Smit, 2009).

In contrast, a second theoretical branch referred to as unit-level constructivism pays more attention to international actors such as states and focuses on the legal and social norms developed within them (ibid.). To bridge the two approaches, the third branch, known as holistic constructivism, uses the concept of ideational structure, while at the same time reflecting on social change and the impact of human agency (ibid.).

Although there are multiple divisions and branches of constructivist theory, the School's essence of philosophy can be summarized under three logics: consequences, appropriateness, and arguing. Firstly, the logic of consequences makes the claim of rational consequentialism, under which a certain action is bound to generate a specific outcome (Krasner, 1999). Hence, people choose to act according to the results they expect to produce, formulating human activity accordingly. In contrast, the logic of appropriateness emphasizes the impact of social practices and norms in shaping human activity. According to this logic, human activity is instead affected by a societal normative framework that indicates what is appropriate and acceptable to do (Onuf, 1995). March and Olsen (2008) discuss the logic of appropriateness as rule-based action, fulfilling the obligations incorporated within social roles, identities, and institutional or political memberships. Müller (2004) and Risse (2000) introduce the third and most recent of these logics, the logic of argument. A meta-theoretical and postmodernist logic, the logic of argument supports that if an argument is convincing and accepted over other arguments, then it can shape human activity, regardless of whether it is objectively correct. When human activity is defined by "the better argument" (Müller, 2004: 397), if parties engage in communication with a readiness to accept the better argument, it can contradict both one's rational interests – logic of consequences – as well as normative structures and social practices – logic of appropriateness (Risse, 2000).

The middle ground provided by the English School and Constructivism in the study of global affairs can also act as a framework of reference for the reconceptualization of tourist activity. Looking at tourism from the English School perspective – or multiple perspectives within the theory – one component to highlight is that the world is a society of states, within which states as political entities coexist and interact with one another. This approach, although heavily state-centric, can explain international tourist activity as one of the many forms of interaction between individuals as ambassadors of states – an activity that falls within the spectrum of public diplomacy.

The English School's universalist approaches provided by solidarist thinkers move beyond state-oriented philosophy. The theory's cosmopolitan underpinnings enable it to view tourism as an organic activity that occurs on a global scale and can be further eased through universal values and regulations – or a more cosmopolitan version of the world. With international tourist activity expected to continue its expansion as a form of unrestricted transnational movement, revolutionist streams of the English School provide an appropriate theoretical framework to undertake its examination in the future, as revolutionist English School viewpoints speak of a world society of individuals and echo Kantian cosmopolitanism.

Wendt (1987) highlights that International Relations theories present contrasting perspectives towards the examination of international political discourse, with realist and other positivist streams adopting a structure-oriented approach, and constructivist theorists focusing more on the agents within the international system. Wendt's (1987) structure–agent differentiation is particularly relevant to this study's attentiveness to non-state political actors, and more specifically to the tourist as a non-state political actor. Risse (2007) further expands on the necessity to bring more attention to political agents vs. structures by explaining that twentieth-century literature on transnational actors maintained a focus on state structures, whereas the attitudes and interactions of non-state political actors remained underexplored. Like the English School, Constructivism also provides components of epistemology that are appropriate for the effective examination of the tourist as a non-state political actor.

When it comes to Constructivism, what is emphasized from its ontological, epistemological, and theoretical standpoint is the social construction of norms, regulations, assumptions, beliefs, and values each society adheres to. Understanding tourism from this perspective allows us to see tourist activity as an exchange of norms, a cross-cultural communication that informs individual travellers on the context of their own beliefs and assumptions in reference to those values and norms their host society brings forward. Tourism, therefore, is an ongoing, transnational, inter-societal process through which the individual as a non-state political actor informs and is informed by societal phenomena and dynamics that exist in various patterns across the globe.

Acknowledging notions of interstate equality, inclusion, and emancipation is most effectively achieved through Critical Theory. The theoretical stream was introduced by Robert W. Cox in 1981 and was critical to the assumption that world order remains unchanged over time (Moolakkattu, 2009). According to Devetak (2009), Critical Theory does not take the state as a standard form of political organization and employs three perspectives to reconceptualizing political community: (1) the normative, (2) the sociological, and (3) the praxeological (ibid.). Through the normative dimension, the state is considered an exclusionary political structure, while the sociological one attends to the origins and evolution of the current political system. The praxeological dimension incorporates notions of cosmopolitanism and dialogue and calls for a more inclusive political order that grants agency and emancipation to both advantaged and marginalized political actors.

A key component of Critical Theory is its attention to the epistemological foundations of political activity. How do we know what we know about politics, and are there other perspectives, structures, and assumptions to consider? As Devetak (2009) explains, Critical Theory embraces the evolution of international politics through inclusive, unconstrained dialogue across the entire humanity, by acknowledging both the sociological origins of international political order and the personal bias of the researcher examining it. Critical Theory is also effective in adopting a reflexive character, by questioning existing structures, deconstructing the origins of existing power dynamics, and identifying the role and agency of non-state actors in international politics. The latter characteristic is directly relevant to the understanding of tourism as a form of international relations, and to this end Critical Theory, similarly to the English School and Constructivism, encapsulates epistemological assumptions that establish it as a suitable theoretical framework for examining tourist-performed international political activity.

In line with the basic principles of reflexivity in Critical Theory, placing tourism at the heart of International Relations requires reflection and evaluation over the appropriateness of the epistemological and theoretical approaches employed to perform this scholarly objective. A reconceptualization of conventional theories, as well as entirely new theoretical angles offer a plethora of opportunities for expanding the epistemological and theoretical spectrum of the IR field, and thus more effectively incorporating emergent forms of international relations, such as tourism.

One challenge that recent literature has identified with regards to the theoretical analysis of International Relations is the angle from which this analysis has been conducted. Much of the theory within the field was developed in an exclusively Western perspective and having realized this, scholars today are trying to incorporate non-Western perspectives into the analysis of the field and enable a post-Western IR theory to develop. This has also been referred to as the "global angle" (Acharya, 2014). A risk that lies within this realization is the dichotomy between Western and non-Western perspectives that would further emphasize rather than eliminate the disparity of the two approaches (Aydınlı and Biltekin, 2018). This can be addressed by adopting the term post-Western to describe theoretical frameworks that cross Western and non-Western boundaries of IR theory and research.

Acharya (2014) suggests that to effectively reimagine IR from a global viewpoint, it is important to diffuse norms and ideas in a reciprocal manner across Western and non-Western agents, and not consider non-Western societies as passive "norm takers" (2014: 655). IR scholarship, which has conventionally adopted a Western-oriented perspective, has overlooked the agency of non-Western beliefs, aspirations, and input, creating an imbalanced account of world affairs. Revisiting international relations by paying equal attention to norms from across the world's societies and civilizations can better account for the interaction and coexistence of these societies – which lies at the core of international relations studies. Undoubtedly, and as highlighted from the constructivist theoretical perspective, tourists are catalytic agents for the exchange of norms across societies. Reconceptualizing IR from a global epistemological perspective will thus require acknowledging the tourist agency and its leading role in inter-societal interaction and exchange.

An overview of IR's key theories illustrates that conventional, state-centric theories, such as Realism and Liberalism, are weaker in corresponding to non-state political activity such as tourism. To the contrary, the theories acknowledging the interconnectedness of state and non-state actors on the world stage and the sociological context that influences their decision-making are more able to correspond to contemporary political phenomena. Through this realization, the book's methodological and research design for the effective study of tourism as a form of international relations is illustrated accordingly.

METHODOLOGY

The book draws its ontological and epistemological assumptions from a combination of three International Relations theories: the English School and its notion of a cosmopolitan world order, Constructivism, and its understanding of international relations as a socially constructed dialectical process shaped by the actors involved, and Critical Theory, with its focus on power dynamics, hierarchy, multi-perspectivity, and emancipation. While the English School also incorporates state-oriented strands that restrict its capacity to identify and assess the tourist as a political agent, its revolutionist and solidarist strands incorporate cosmopolitan assumptions that are appropriate within the context of international tourist activity. On the other end, Critical Theory is inherently cosmopolitan, as its reflexive character questions existing structural realities and looks beyond conventional boundaries of political order. These theories provide not only the theoretical framework for discussing tourist activity within the international political arena, but additionally provide recommendations on the methodological directions to be taken in its analysis.

Combining the principal philosophies that emerge from these theories allows a set of assumptions to be made with regards to the international political stage and the role of tourism:

- Positivist and state-oriented assumptions of the international political stage should be deconstructed and re-evaluated to reflect the dynamic and evolving nature of contemporary global affairs.
- International affairs are conducted by an amalgamation of state and non-state actors that share the capacity to shape global phenomena.
- Processes of globalization have drastically expanded the world's interconnectedness and interdependency, to a level that socio-political phenomena occur on a global and not on a national scale.
- Addressing global challenges can be more effective through cosmopolitan rather than state-centric versions of international relations, to provide

unconventional political actors with more agency and make the international political stage more inclusive and effective.

The optimal approach to incorporate these assumptions into the discussion and analysis of this book is by adopting a theoretical angle of critical cosmopolitanism, an approach defined in more detail through Chapter 1. Beck (2007) calls cosmopolitanism the new critical theory of the twenty-first century. Delanty and Harris (2018) highlight the critical angle of cosmopolitanism and present critical cosmopolitanism as a scholarly perspective that wishes to identify the present's transformational capabilities. Informed from a selection of IR theories that each – including Realism and Liberalism – articulates the tourist's political capacities from different angles and to different degrees, critical cosmopolitanism is employed within the context of this book as an inter-theoretical IR framework set to assess an emergent political actor, the tourist, and pave the way for new and more inclusive IR theories to develop.

With critical cosmopolitanism as a reference point of analysis, each book chapter is set to employ additional theoretical models and analytical tools derived from Tourism studies, such as the Push and Pull Factor model (Dann, 1977), models of Tourist Typology (Cohen, 1972; Plog, 1974), and the Big Five categories of personality – as employed for tourist behaviour (McCrae and Costa, 1985). The book utilizes contemporary examples and case studies to provide practical insights and give context to theoretical discussions. Through this methodological approach, the reader has access to insights, practices, and phenomena that advance this notion of multi-perspectivity.

OVERVIEW AND STRUCTURE

Non-state actors have emerged in contemporary IR research as catalytic players in the international political and economic stage. Chapter 1 discusses tourism as a non-state actor to identify the influence of global tourist activity on international development and sustainable practice. The chapter places the theoretical framework of cosmopolitanism at the forefront and examines cosmopolitan forms of tourism in association with sustainable development. Through the case studies the chapter presents, it highlights global power dynamics and opportunities for tourism to either emancipate or disadvantage marginalized populations. More specifically, it discusses the forms of tourist activity that bring advantaged, high-income visitors to communities of disadvantaged populations living under the poverty line – a type of global intergroup interaction that may generate patterns of oppression or leave room for unethical, non-consensual interaction between hosts and visitors. The notion of critical cosmopolitanism provides an insight as to how this intergroup exchange can generate empowerment rather than prejudice. Looking at tourism as a catalytic activity for developing intergroup relations of inequality on a global scale suggests that tourism can also be seen as a tool for global governance and international development.

The discussion on tourism, cosmopolitanism, and international development is followed by an overview of international security and its evolution in Chapter 2. This chapter, titled "Tourism and diplomacy", focuses on the act of international diplomacy in reference to the stakeholders performing it and distinguishes between two categories of diplomatic discourse. The first one is state-oriented diplomacy, undertaken either by state or non-state actors to advance the interests of state actors, their image abroad, and their foreign policy. The second one is cosmopolitan diplomacy, which, like state-oriented diplomacy, can be performed by both state and non-state political actors. Cosmopolitan diplomacy addresses international political affairs from a transnational rather than a state-oriented angle to resolve global challenges and enable political agents to coordinate their efforts irrespectively of their national affiliations. The distinction between state-oriented and cosmopolitan diplomacy is employed to discuss the ways in which tourism informs contemporary diplomacy, and how tourist-performed diplomacy engages unconventional actors in the act of political negotiation both as representatives of institutions or organized communities, as well as in their capacity as individual travellers.

Chapter 3 on "Tourism and international security" offers a timeline of international events that shaped perceptions and measures towards international security, while discussing how international tourist activity affected and was affected by these events. An initial point of reference is the end of the Cold War, discussed through a selection of key texts on the implications of the post-Cold War era towards globalization, interconnectedness, and travel. This is followed by a discussion on the case study of the 9/11 attacks and the War on Terror, with the significant changes that were imposed on security screenings for cross-border travel. A third key reference is the COVID-19 pandemic and how international security is redefined through the threat of a global health crisis. The chapter assesses the role of international tourist activity in shaping five key areas of international security: the military, the political, the societal, the environmental, and the economic.

With an understanding of how tourism can be a driver of sustainable development, an unconventional actor in diplomacy, and a determinant of international security, Chapter 4 proceeds to discuss the popular relationship between Tourism and Peace and consider the ways in which tourism can be a contributor to peace within – but more so beyond – the framework of conflict resolution. With numerous scholarly accounts attempting to establish and measure the relationship between tourist activity and the successful implementation of sustainable peace, this chapter deviates from the question "Does tourism lead to peace?" and instead asks "Which forms of tourism contribute to peace and how?". These questions are addressed by going beyond the establishment of peace through processes of conflict resolution to consider indirect routes to peace, such as though development, security, and diplomacy.

CONCLUSION

International Relations is a historically state-centric field moving beyond state actors and attempting to understand international affairs more holistically and comprehensively from a multitude of angles. To view tourism through International Relations requires first to identify the approaches used within the field for examining and analysing the world. This allows us to identify current viewpoints, perspectives, and assumptions within the field of International Relations, acknowledge them as part of the author's starting point, and apply this lens in the discussion of international and contemporary tourist activity.

To see tourism beyond its capacity as an industry performing transnational economic activity allows scholars to directly embrace the complexity and multifaceted nature of tourism. Acknowledging its socio-economic nature provides an opportunity to identify and measure tourism's contribution to global phenomena and dynamics, and to consider individual tourists as potential non-state actors with the ability to engage in and shape international affairs.

With this objective in mind, it is imperative that this book adopts appropriate ontological, epistemological, and theoretical frameworks. Through a review of prominent IR theories, this chapter differentiates between state-centric and cosmopolitan frameworks, deeming the latter as more appropriate in identifying, discussing, and evaluating tourists as emergent non-state political actors. To this end, employing a critical theoretical angle to cosmopolitanism enables the analysis of the tourist as a non-state actor to deconstruct conventional assumptions in international relations, critique relationships of inequality and injustice, and seek for the avenues that enable the recognition and empowerment of historically overlooked political agents.

Why is tourism an international socio-political activity worth exploring? The exponential growth of this activity of voluntary transnational movement is here to stay, even after a severe pandemic. Tourism is becoming more frequent, more widespread, and even more embedded in our everyday lifestyle across Western, Westernized, and non-Western societies. This activity is also influenced by our constant exposure to news and information from across the globe and our access to social media platforms that engage everyday citizens in politically informed communication. It is, therefore, more likely for the contemporary tourist today to perform travel not solely as a leisure activity to escape the daily routine, but as a politically informed and even politically driven activity that enhances cosmopolitan values, in an era when our lifestyles are already shaped by global phenomena beyond our doorstep. Through the theoretical angle of critical cosmopolitanism, this book is set to reveal those forms of tourism that are expected to have significant contributions to international affairs and evaluate the nature of these contributions as they are introduced through the widened scope of the new International Relations.

In its diversity of forms, tourism as a political act can yield socio-political implications through a diversity of international political processes. The quest for sustainable development, coordinated global action, diplomatic communication across political actors, and measures for increased international security are only a few of the areas of international political discourse that can engage tourists as non-state political contributors. Through the lens of critical cosmopolitanism, the following chapters examine international tourism trends and redefine tourist activity within the facets of international development, diplomacy, international security, and peace. To commence this discussion, the following chapter introduces a spectrum of tourist typologies and discusses how each engages with notions of sustainable development, as well as transnational and intergenerational equity.

1. Tourism and international development

AN INTRODUCTION TO INTERNATIONAL DEVELOPMENT

The study of International Development has been closely linked to economic growth and has, often exclusively, been assessed through economic terms. Defining development is a challenging task and one that has yielded over 70 different definitions as development studies progressed through the years (Sharpley, 2000). This has led scholars to bestow various meanings to the term as they apply it to a range of contexts across disciplines. Todaro and Smith (2009) attempt to capture the multifaceted character of development through the following definition:

> Development [is] a multidimensional process involving major changes in social structures, popular attitudes, and national institutions, as well as the acceleration of economic growth, the reduction of inequality and the eradication of poverty. Development, in its essence, must represent the whole gamut of change by which an entire social system, tuned to the diverse basic needs and desires of individuals and social groups within that system, moves away from a condition of life widely perceived as unsatisfactory toward a situation or condition of life regarded as materially and spiritually better.

Todaro and Smith's (2009) definition speaks of a life spiritually and materially better through indicators of economic growth, poverty reduction and – economic – inequality. According to Daly (2006), development is defined as global economic growth. The conventional focus of development scholars on economic factors and indicators has, until recently, overlooked the parameters of environmental sustainability and – to some extent – social equity. The three pillars of the environment, the economy, and society are principal determinants in making development processes sustainable. Today, the concept of sustainable development has gained significant attention in development scholarship and is a concept that proposes achieving economic growth while ensuring environmental conservation and societal welfare.

Alkire (2010) discusses the notion of human development and offers a human-centred approach to development that deviates from economic indicators: human development is about expanding people's freedoms and addresses three objectives in doing so: (1) well-being, (2) agency, and (3) justice. Development can be understood both as an end goal and as a process (Sharpley, 2000); it is a process that continues to improve living conditions, choices, and freedoms in societies across the world, and at the same time the process is comprised of agreed developmental landmarks and outputs that make progress measurable and time-specific. Evidently, the end goal of development is the advancement of individuals as distinct units and of society on a collective scale, with economic performance service as one of multiple indicators towards achieving this goal.

Approaches to the study and examination of development have evolved over the decades, with a set of development paradigms illustrating the evolution of development theory. Two prominent development paradigms that emerged in the 1950s and 1960s are the *modernization* and *dependency* paradigms, that focus on indicators of economic growth (Telfer, 2002). The modernization paradigm uses Western development stages as points of reference applicable on both Western and non-Western societies globally, whereas the dependency paradigm acknowledges that colonialism and structures of global economic activity have enabled developed nations to exploit developing ones and result in their under-development (ibid.). According to Telfer's (2015) evolution of development theory, these models were replaced by the model of *economic Neoliberalism* in the 1970s, characterized by economic deregulation and free market policies. Around the same period, the model of *alternative development* also emerged and introduced a less economic-centric approach to development, incorporating social and environmental parameters such as education, shelter, health, gender equality, people empowerment through grassroot movements, and sustainability (ibid.). The model of alternative development is considered, as Sharpley (2000: 6) puts it, "the current end-point of the development paradigm continuum".

Today, the examination of development entails the component of sustainability; for any developmental process and goal to be considered successful, they ought to entail durability across time and refrain from any counter side effects. International development should therefore be assessed with regards to economic, social, and environmental outputs. Yet to jointly pursue economic development and resource conservation has been viewed as an oxymoron and an unrealistic goal (Sharpley, 2000). Nevertheless, it is equally unrealistic that to aspire to long-term economic development without ensuring resource availability and quality of life might also be seen as an evident oxymoron, making economic development achievable only in the short run.

Development and Globalization

Looking at international development from an International Relations perspective, the examination of development was directly affected by the realization that the post-Cold War international political arena was becoming increasingly interconnected. IR research during the 1990s and thereafter was heavily centred around speculations of the political order that would replace the world's bipolar structure (Fukuyama, 1989; Huntington, 1993), while social and economic studies of the time were discussing how post-Cold War realities would shape development and power dynamics on a global scale (Ritzer, 1992; Brown and Lauder, 1996). A common acknowledgement across scholarship in the social sciences was that the world was characterized by increased interconnectedness, interdependence, and increased global access; this process was labelled *globalization*.

While the dawn of the post-Cold War era revealed a world that was more politically stable and safer to navigate, the processes of globalization that were underway were flagged as threatening to non-Western socio-political and cultural authenticity. Smith (2018) admits that globalization was heavily US-led, and as such it was a one-way relationship of spreading global capitalism and engaging non-Western societies in processes of assimilation. What was initially labelled as globalization was in fact an unfiltered process of spreading the world's dominant political and economic ideologies and cultural practices; a phenomenon soon redefined as Americanization (Smith, 2018), McDonaldization (Ritzer, 1992), and Westernization (Bozkurt, 2012). While Americanization described globalization as a US-initiated spread of socio-political, cultural, and economic trends, the term Westernization placed the phenomenon within the broader Western civilization and labelled it as the spread of Western values and ideas over non-Western practices.

A key component of Westernization and the global spread of American ideologies was the capitalist ideology of free trade – an ideology that advocated for less governmental regulations and more open competition across businesses, suppliers, products, and service providers. The post-Cold War globalized era featured a global spread of free trade, capitalist ideologies, and transnational economic activity. As such, alongside the socio-political changes delivered by globalization, a notable change is observed in international economic processes. An iconic account of this new reality was provided by Thomas Friedman's *The World is Flat* (2005), which highlighted the international co-dependency of economic processes, the global competitiveness of products and services, and the inevitability of a global economic shift towards this direction.

Globalization undoubtedly came with practical and visible societal changes. McDonaldization, an equally popular term in the study of globalization, was used to emphasize the spread of US-based fast-food culture, embodying not only fast-paced urban environments, but also heavy standardization of culinary experiences (Ritzer, 1992). The standardized American fast-food experience was soon available on a global scale, and particularly through the tourist segments of cities and destinations – otherwise referred to as tourist bubbles. An analogous process of standardization was also adopted by international hotel franchises which, in addition to fast-food chains, comprised most of a tourist bubble's infrastructure.

TOURISM IN THE ERA OF GLOBALIZATION

As a multifaceted and ongoing process, globalization has been central to the evolution of international tourist activity in the post-Cold War era and beyond. While the end of the Cold War and the fall of the Berlin Wall eased and enabled travel across Soviet-aligned and Western-aligned territories from a perspective of political security, additional advancements in the areas of technology and transportation made travel easier, more frequently attainable, and gradually more affordable. For the aspiring traveller, the world started to appear more accessible, even its mysterious or lesser-known corners. The evolution of internet technologies and the web became a primary reference point for gathering information for potential destinations and minimizing the risk of the unknown. Globalization thus was not only characterized by the expansion of a prevalent western political ideology internationally that monopolized global politics, but it also enabled the voluminous exchange of information at a global scale, shaping tourist decision-making in unprecedented ways.

Understanding tourist behaviour and its evolution during the past five decades starts from the conception of tourist typologies that Cohen (1972) and Plog (1974) delivered in the early 1970s. The two scholars provide a spectrum of tourist behaviour that predicts tourist activity based on tourist psychographic information and individual preferences. At one end of the spectrum lie tourists with little interest in novelty and a strong preference for familiarity. Plog (1974, 2001) identified this end of the spectrum as the *dependable* and *psychocentric* tourists, who are more cautious and conservative towards their travel choices and depend on tourist infrastructure to ensure a more passive and accustomed experience. Cohen (1972) calls this tourist typology as the *organized mass tourist.* At the opposite end of the spectrum, Cohen presents the *drifter*, and Plog the *venturer* – or *allocentric* – tourist, who share similar characteristics and travel choices. The drifter seeks the authenticity of novelty, prefers to move outside the tourist zones of destinations, and is attracted by the adventure attached to an open and flexible itinerary. Within the same context of preferences, Plog's venturer and allocentric tourists are curious, driven by a desire to explore and actively engage with new – and hidden – destinations as appealing fresh products on the marketplace. They are confident of their own assessment capabilities and avoid any reliance on tourist providers. Within the middle of the spectrum lie consecutively Cohen's *individual mass tourist* and the *explorer*, respectively to Plog's *mid-centric* tourist, the *near dependable*, and the *near venturer* as shown in Figure 1.1.

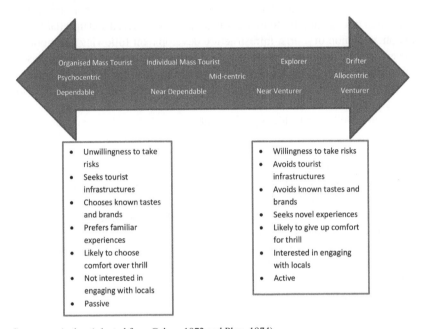

Source: Author (adapted from Cohen, 1972 and Plog, 1974).

Figure 1.1   A spectrum of tourist typologies

Using this spectrum of tourist motivation and preferences as a reference point allows the tourism scholar to see how trends in tourist activity shifted over the years and moved from the left side of the spectrum to the right.

The tourist bubble, or the designated tourist zone of destinations, is the popular choice for psychocentric visitors and organized mass tourists. They provide a safety net over the uncertainty of novelty. Cohen (1972) introduces the phenomenon of the *tourist environmental bubble* as the familiar microenvironment that the tourist remains confined within for the duration of their time abroad; one that resembles home to the greatest extent possible. The standardized nature of tourist bubbles, being comprised primarily of international food and hotel chains, created a direct association to globalization, with tourist bubbles being regarded as yet another product of Westernization and standardization in tourism. Interestingly, the phenomenon of tourist bubbles emerged during the 1970s (Cohen, 1972; Stors and Kagermeier, 2013), when the lack of information, online connectivity, and instant news left new destinations in the shadows. Urban environments across the US – where this trend began – appeared as threatening crime hubs, inhospitable to the visitor (ibid.). One can therefore argue that standardization emerged in a pre-globalization era, when information for tourist destinations was scattered and unreliable. Yet the phenomenon of tourist infrastructure development following the model of the environmental bubble continued until today, at a time when the expansion of information and the increase in available outlets has led to an increase in familiarity with new destinations and to the formation of more realistic expectations.

Cohen (2008), alongside a plethora of other scholars, has flagged globalization as a key determinant of the standardization of destinations, their commodification, and consequently their loss of authenticity. While authenticity is difficult to identify and measure, particularly for "immaterial elements" such as tourist experiences (Heitmann, 2011: 45), it is seen as a primary factor in tourist motivation and decision-making (MacCannell, 1973; Waller and Lea, 1999; Nguyen and Cheung, 2016). The search for authenticity as a principal motivator in tourism encouraged destinations to "bring" authenticity to the visitor and produce staged or Westernized versions of authenticity for tourist consumption. While this phenomenon was detected in the early 1970s (McCannell, 1973) and as such was not an outcome of post-Cold War globalization, processes of post-Cold War standardization were linked to staged and commodified versions of culture, a process that Solomon (2015) referred to as authenticity simulation for the post-tourist. Ironically, the centrality of authenticity in post-modern tourist experiences led to the in-authentication of authentic experiences through their commodification.

Can one argue that post-Westernized destinations are less authentic? Perhaps the sight of familiar brands and standardized services, processes, and flavours comes to contest local tastes, customs, and dynamics. Additionally, simulated and commodified cultures within tourist zones are far from organic cultural performances and illustrations. Authenticity, however, has also been sought beyond tourist zones and outside of tourist bubbles, not only in the performance and illustration of inherited cultural rituals and customs, but also in the organic embodiment of contemporary aspects of culture in a destination, such as contemporary lifestyles, fusion cuisines, locally adapted global trends, contemporary music, film, and arts. While forms of cultural expression across destinations may have evolved and been influenced by globalization, Americanization, and Westernization, there is a distinction to be made between globalized cultures and cultures staged solely for the purpose of tourist consumption.

Scholarship raised the concern of cultural assimilation as a phenomenon driven by international tourist demand in the era of globalization. At the same time, it acknowledges the contribution of globalization in forming new markets and making new tourist experiences available (Dwyer, 2015). Interestingly, new market realities and its opportunities left room for market segmentation to occur. Tourists started travelling not only through pre-arranged organized packages, but according to individual interests and personal desires. The same destination would accept visitors for different purposes, ranging from culture-oriented travel to educational tourism, or for visiting friends and relatives (VFR). The segmentation of the market revealed the plethora of preferences and motivations behind the tourist's decision-making process, illustrating more clearly than ever before Cohen's and Plog's tourist typologies.

Globalization has enabled tourists to deviate from the organized mass tourist model and adopt more allocentric behaviours, customizing their own travel experiences and daring to navigate beyond the tourist bubble (Stors and Kagermeier, 2013). As tourism was reinvented and reconceptualized throughout the years, the realities globalization created enabled an increased sense of safety and familiarity with novel destinations, shifted tourist activity trends towards the drifter end of the tourist typology spectrum, and enabled the unconventional exploration of new destinations beyond designated zones of tourist infrastructure. Reconceptualizing the contribution of globalization to tourism from the angle of information provision and not from the standardization perspective redefines the tourist's exposure to authenticity and culture.

Today, the inevitability of an interconnected world as projected in the 1990s has been thoroughly reaffirmed. The decades that followed the end of the Cold War reinforced the trends of globalization by making the world even smaller, and even more accessible. They were characterized by increased diversification of air transportation options, including an increase in air travel suppliers, and a wider range of prices – including lower fare options. In addition to evident changes in the frequency of travel and the availability of destinations, tourism observed a shift in the ways travellers chose to engage with their destination. While tourist activity in the 1990s was primarily performed through the organized, visual consumption of destinations – with Urry (1990) coining the term *the tourist gaze* to describe this phenomenon – the globalized, or post-modern tourist sought for more performative, hands-on, experiential ways of engaging with short-term travel. Everett (2008: 337) explains that post-modern tourists pursue "embodied experiences", in contrast with the tourism of visual and passive consumption of previous decades. While in the twentieth century, the conventional tourist sought a venue of escaping the fast-paced industrialized Fordist lifestyle by accessing exotic and romanticized settings (Dujmović and Vitasović, 2015), the tourist of the twenty-first century engages in frequent travel for multiple purposes (leisure and non-leisure), shifting travel from a purpose of escapism to making it part of one's routine and fast-paced lifestyle. The tourist in post-modernity, or the post-tourist, is one that finds authenticity through organic interactions with the locals and one that achieves a sense of locality away from tourist infrastructure and tourist-specific affiliations.

Whether a destructive or beneficial force, globalization's catalytic role in the evolution of international tourist activity is indisputable. The transnational interconnectedness of the world became even more evident in the years of the COVID-19 pandemic, which erupted in 2020 and spread on a global scale within a matter of weeks. The globalized world, which holds the ability to share instant information, global accessibility, and increased mobility, was also catalytic in enabling the COVID-19 virus to become a pandemic (Ducharme, 2020). As a response, a political act taken to halt the spread of the virus was to impose travel restrictions across national and intrastate borders, forcibly minimizing tourist activity on a global scale. Transnational, intercultural, and any form of distant physical interaction and contact was interrupted in search of a medical response to the pandemic, which came approximately a year afterwards through globally available vaccination (European Commission, 2020). On the brink of 2022, and with global vaccination well underway, the pandemic is still an ongoing health threat, yet projections on post-pandemic travel are starting to emerge. The projections agree that transnational mobility and short-term travel will resurface as an integral component of contemporary lifestyle; however, a renewed appreciation of the ability to travel may prioritize certain forms of tourism over others. Carbone (2020) and Antoniou (2021) project that post-pandemic trends in tourism will be anthropocentric, while forms of tourism that promote individual well-being or societal development will be prioritized over superficial and consumption-oriented engagements with destinations.

Following decades of evident globalization with both positive and negative outcomes, the question one ought to ask today is how to enable the positive and productive elements of globalization to flourish, minimize the negative, and conduct globalization ethically for the mutual benefit of all actors affected. Globalization can be delivered in a healthier and more sustainable – and eman-cipatory – manner, by shifting it from the one-way communication process that was described as Americanization and Westernization, to a reciprocal, two-way exchange of information (Smith, 2018). In doing so, it is important to conceptualize the world as one unit of interconnected and interdependent equal parts. An effective scholarly approach that achieves this worldview – and can assist in redefining the world through universal values and mutual benefits for all – is cosmopolitanism.

COSMOPOLITANISM AND INTERNATIONAL GOVERNANCE

Linklater (2009) defines cosmopolitanism as a world order where universal moral values are adhered to and the gap between domestic and international politics is minimized. An initial conceptualization of cosmopolitanism, which then gave way to additional variations of the term, was coined by Kant, and finds its roots in the IR theory of Liberalism as a notion of cosmopolitan democracy enabled through regional bodies and institutions (Burchill, 2009). The essence of cosmopolitanism lies at the philosophy of world citizenship, being citizens of a joint *cosmos* that connects beyond state boundaries.

Cosmopolitanism is the notion of political governance and world order that looks beyond state loyalty and state boundedness and has been conceptualized from a variety of standpoints within IR theory. Critical theory refers to the concept of *thin cosmopolitanism*, which acknowledges that loyalty to the state exists, but it is not absolute. If a state-centric world order gives moral hierarchy to the state, thin cosmopolitanism suggests that there is no fixed hierarchy of allegiance to the state versus loyalty to humanity globally. Critical theory speaks of thin cosmopolitanism as an expanded political community beyond the state (Devetak, 2009), a notion analogous to the English School's international society, characterized by cosmopolitan culture and modernity. As Devetak (2009) admits, a cosmopolitan world order implies that the state is no longer the central actor and agent of international political organization. From the English School perspective, Linklater (2009) admits a growing demand for what Bull (1984) had previously referred to as cosmopolitan moral awareness, considering increased concerns for individual human rights that have put the right to state sovereignty in question. Principal English School figures Bull and Wight agree that cosmopolitanism is about the importance of all states and international actors being on the same page, or effectively adopting a common framework of universal values.

Latour (2004) moves beyond thin cosmopolitanism to suggest that thinking of a common world is inaccurate, as there is no collective understanding or a universal viewpoint of the world, or *cosmos*. Therefore, thinking of multiple worlds – or multiple perspectives – coexisting is more appropriate. Blaser (2016) highlights Latour's and Stengers' contributions to the study of cosmopolitanism, as they deviate away from the notion of universal values, or common worldviews, and instead discuss the process through which divergent political values can coexist in a stable yet diverse common world. The process of creating a common cosmos is referred to as cosmopolitics, and it has come to the forefront of international politics through phenomena of increased inter-connectedness and globalization.

If the goal of cosmopolitics is to achieve peaceful coexistence among diverse agents in an increasingly globalized world of unavoidable coexistence, the practice of global governance comes into question. Discussing global governance has become inevitable as emergent global issues and new actors in international affairs transcend state boundaries and reaffirm a global interdependence. Finkelstein (1995) speaks of an internationalization of challenges to human rights and democracy, which were previously considered state-bound issues. Finkelstein (ibid.: 368) reiterates that the world in the post-Cold War era is an "expanding universe of actors, issues, and activities", and global governance is what occurs in the absence of a world government. This is exponentially more evident today, approximately three decades after Finkelstein's 1995 realization. Global governance is exercised by actors with global influence, both state and non-state ones.

It is, therefore, possible for tourists as non-state agents of international affairs to influence processes of global governance and contribute to the process of cosmopolitics, for shaping a more cosmopolitan world of shared – or different yet respected – values. According to Molz (2006), aspects of cosmopolitanism such as adaptability and openness are best embodied by mobile individuals, such as tourists. To that end, tourism embodies cosmopolitanism, and due to this embodiment, cosmopolitanism escapes the abstract character it assumes in the absence of a concrete global governance framework. While Molz (ibid.) calls Kant's notion of a global citizenship utopian and current understandings of cosmopolitanism as typified and idealized, she advocates that cosmopolitanism can be materialized and can escape its "detached idealization" (ibid.: 2) by revisiting its applicability through the act of tourism.

Critical Cosmopolitanism through Tourism

Swain (2009) discusses the contribution of tourism to cosmopolitanism as a hopeful pursuit that has the potential to generate positive outputs. Tourism, as an interactive activity between hosts and visitors at an expansive international scale, holds the capacity to foster both oppressive and empowering relations across these two groups. As Swain (ibid.) explains, tourism as an international practice embraces cosmopolitan ideas. Yet, some argue that upholding these values is not a prerequisite for travel, and thus there is a possibility for tourist activity to move towards oppressive dynamics and cultivate power imbalances and inequalities.

Relationships of inequality across hosts and visitors are not uncommon, especially when visitors of developed, technologically advanced, and high-income nations meet host communities in developing, low-income communities. As Urry (1996) highlighted in the 1990s, the visual consumption of the host by the visitor in the form of the tourist gaze highlighted patterns of social inequality, particularly when members of non-industrialized communities were seen as the exotic native. An emblematic characteristic of the tourist gaze was the collection of photographs – often with an assumed or involuntary consent by the host communities. Urry (ibid.) also gives the example of sexual gazing at Asian girls by male visitors, which illustrates a power imbalance not only in economic or national terms, but also in the aspect of gender.

Phillips et al. (2021) use critical discourse analysis to highlight how Western outlets romanticize poverty and inequality in non-Western, developing destinations, such as Fiji, and prolong colonial stereotypes of happy, colourful and exotic, uneducated natives. A risky pattern arises when, in developing destinations such as non-industrialized Pacific islands, economic inequality and the status of developing economics becomes linked to authenticity and timelessness. If locals of these destinations were to engage in industrialized or technologically advanced sectors and escape the image of a hospitable, non-urbanized native, they would somehow lose their authenticity – an authenticity granted to the hosts by the Western standards of visitors.

In an analogous case, Western tourists rushed to visit Cuba in the 2010s before the island state embraced a more capitalist and commercialized character – a projection that was fuelled when the Obama administration took steps to ease restrictions to Cuba, restoring their diplomatic relations and enabling commercial flights and cruise ships from the US to Cuba; steps that allowed tourism to increase exponentially. As travel blogger Vicky Brown mentions in a pre-pandemic article on tourism to Cuba, "communism slowly eases its grip on Cuba, allowing imported technology and private enterprise, [and] there is an increasing sense amongst travellers that you must 'go there now, before it all changes'". Visitors were eager to visit and access the "*real*" Cuba before losing its authenticity through economic advancements, urbanization, and increased opportunities of cross-cultural exchanges. The authenticity of Cuba from this Western visitor perspective was directly associated with the embargo status of the nation, and the fact that the state of limbo the local population was in for decades, preventing international trade and development, was romanticized as authentic culture to the eyes of urbanized, advantaged visitors.

Visiting the disadvantaged: slum and volunteer tourism

The unequal relationship between urbanized visitors and struggling hosts, accompanied by a reconceptualization of poverty and inequality as romanticized simplicity and an opportunity for resourcefulness, is further exacerbated in the case of slum tourism, for which the destinations of slums provide visitors with access to conditions of extreme impoverishment, over-crowdedness, and questionable shelter and sanitation.

According to Nisbett (2017) the issue of romanticizing poverty – a condition that endangers lives and is linked to political decisions and international relations – starts from treating impoverished communities as a phenomenon that simply exists. The tourist detaches themselves from the politics of poverty and treats it as an externally developed reality with no political character. The western tourist assumes the role of an observer that simply passes by to visually consume poverty as a ground-breaking, life-changing experience, but without engaging directly with it. Nevertheless, slums are a vivid representation of the international patterns of extreme economic inequality, and as such their up-close examination by members of wealthier societies is a political act.

India, a country of over a billion inhabitants, is a primary example of intra-state economic inequality, and is home to multiple, densely populated slums. Dharavi is an internationally known slum in Mumbai, that receives frequent foreign visitors through organized tours. A simple search online markets Dharavi as Asia's largest slum, an authentic location from the internationally known film *Slumdog Millionaire*, and offers a plethora of options for booking a tour of the slum. While the ethics of marketing the visual consumption of impoverished communities in the Global South by economically independent visitors from the Global North are put in question, the main tour operator for Dharavi's slum tourism, *Reality Tours*, claims to address concerns of unethical engagement with slums by using mechanisms that bring slum tourism profits back into the community (Nisbett, 2017; Reality Tours and Travel, 2020).

When viewing tourism as a non-politicized act, one can argue that slum visitors are simply observers of the phenomenon of poverty generated by global economic policies and local governance inadequacy. On the other hand, slum tourism becomes a political act by commercializing and romanticizing poverty to advantaged, wealthy visitors and leaving impoverished hosts as disempowered subjects in an exchange of benign power imbalance that reaffirms and extenuates the factors that lead to this vast economic divergence. According to Nisbett (2017), Dharavi is presented as a business hub, with handcrafted products provided to visitors, and visitors seeing it less as an impoverished community and more as an economically active community that they can contribute to. This perspective allows the Western visitors to perceive their engagement with the slum as positive and depoliticize their slum tourism experience by ignoring phenomena of extreme poverty and injustice (ibid.). Nisbett (2017: 43) reviewed opinions from slum tourists to Dharavi that found the experience life-changing and eye-opening, an observation that, as the author admits, shows that slum tourism empowers "the wrong people", the "privileged white, Western middle classes" and not the slum inhabitants.

From an analogous standpoint, volunteer tourism – or voluntourism – comes to merge the Global North with the Global South with what is theoretically a relationship of giving to the disadvantaged; a form of tourism that escapes the passive visual consumption and ad-hoc economic support of slum tourism by directly addressing the needs of disadvantaged and impoverished communities. Yet, like slum tourism, it is questionable whether volunteer tourism is about offering to the community more than it is about transforming and empowering the visitor through an out-of-the-ordinary experience. Superficial and controversial applications of voluntourism have resulted in the display of extraordinary travel as an achievement by young, white, Western visitors; a display that does not guarantee fruitful contributions to the communities visited. University students taking a break from school to do good in a less developed community are not necessarily equipped with the knowledge, skills, and cultural familiarity with their destination of choice to deliver socially sustainable results. Blogs, talks, and opinion articles have criticized the superficiality of volunteer tourism as an extracurricular learning experience and not as an act of meaningful philanthropy (Rosenberg, 2018; Nedyalkov, 2019). Others also make mention of the white saviour complex, or the perception of advantaged, white, Western voluntourists that they know how to save a challenged community without necessarily working alongside the locals to help them craft sustainable solutions (Biddle, 2014; Gould, 2019).

McGehee (2014) asks whether voluntourism is about altruism or about self-development. Luh Sin et al. (2015) view volunteer tourism as a social and political phenomenon that reflects worldviews and ethical predispositions. With the popularity and frequency of volunteer tourism on the rise, it has come to be considered a new non-state form of international development, giving agency to volunteer tourists as shapers of global socio-economic realities and potential contributors to social justice (ibid.). Volunteer tourism is, therefore, theoretically expected to contribute to international development and social justice; yet, in practice, it is uncertain whether individuals who undertake voluntourism are motivated by a sense of altruism or a focus on personal transformation. McGehee (2014) notes that acknowledging the expectations of volunteer tourists to engage in transformational experiences should not be overlooked, and with appropriate mechanisms, voluntourism can become an ultimate form of sustainable tourism, contributing positively to hosts and visitors alike, and embracing their environmental, social, and economic sustainability.

Tourist–host interaction: under what conditions?
Unequal interaction across people and communities runs an elevated risk of breeding animosity and contributing to negative stereotypes, prejudice, and hostility (Allport, 1954). Unequal interaction between hosts and visitors, or tourists and the local population, can lead to controversy and antagonism (Swain, 2009). A pre-condition for tourism as a contributor to social justice and international development should be tourist activity to be conducted on equal and reciprocal terms, providing agency to both hosts and visitors and ensuring consent by those directly or otherwise involved. According to Swain

(2009), critical cosmopolitan theory is an appropriate theoretical spectrum for understanding and advancing the political influences of international tourist activity and gearing tourism towards a more equal world of "hope".

To identify and isolate relationships of inequality allows tourism scholars and practitioners to encourage tourist activity that empowers over tourist activity that oppresses. According to Swain (2009), the critical application of cosmopolitanism can ensure that international tourist activity enables equality, emancipation, and empowerment, over continuing and reinforcing global inequalities. Critical cosmopolitanism establishes the conditions in which tourists can embody and perform cosmopolitics and contribute to individuals' abilities to "understand each other and create equitable lives" (ibid.: 505) on a global scale.

Globalization is a key phenomenon to acknowledge when discussing cosmopolitan political activity and more specifically when applying critical cosmopolitanism in tourism. Globalization has set the stage for international political activity to occur; a stage characterized by high interconnectivity, interdependency, but also an unequal balance of power across Western and non-Western societies. According to Swain (2009), applying critical cosmopolitanism in the contemporary globalized world creates opportunities for shifting unbalanced power dynamics by promoting global citizenship, human rights, and cultural diversity. This abstract vision becomes more applicable through tourist activity. Tourism can affect attitudes, transform destinations, and shape cultural practice by enabling the organic amalgamation of host and tourist worldviews. It can yield transformational experiences to hosts and visitors alike, and to this end tourism assumes the ability to shape worldviews.

Critical cosmopolitanism acknowledges multiple stakeholders in tourism – not a simple binary relationship between hosts and visitors. The multi-perspectivity of stakeholders in tourism more effectively grasps both Western and non-Western perspectives, allowing a plethora of opinions and voices to be heard on an international scale, including previously marginalized voices by disadvantaged host communities. Examples of slum and volunteer tourist activity have illustrated that tourist interactions between members of advantaged and disadvantaged communities are prone to unequal and unethical interactions, in which host communities become commodified for privileged visitors, and consent is problematic. Yet encounters between the Global North and Global South can be ethical, if the tourist activity ensures consent by host stakeholders involved and enables them to equally shape their interaction – a point also raised by Swain (2009).

At the same time, tourist expectations of authenticity in a visited destination should realistically depict contemporary dynamics of that community, instead of a romanticized, non-industrialized version of an isolated community of *natives*. Experiencing an interconnected and globalized world of constant technological advancements, while expecting *exotic* destinations to remain unchanged, can be a utopian expectation and can create a harmful demand for tourism-dependent destinations to force a false version of where their culture and authenticity lie. On the other hand, escaping colonial expectations of what exotic destinations should portray, it is possible for cultural exchanges through tourist activity to adopt an ethical character and occur under conditions of equal, respectful, and reciprocal encounters, allowing host and tourist stakeholders alike to acquire positive depictions of the other's culture.

While Swain (2009) insightfully presents tourism as a mechanism for achieving critical cosmopolitanism for a world of fewer inequalities, Johnson (2014) further details how this can be measured more effectively, enabling cosmopolitan action through tourism to adopt a more applicable and comprehensible form. Johnson argues that *cultural literacy* is an interpretive analytical tool that can address the gap Swain (2009) identifies in cosmopolitan methodology. She provides a traditional and a contemporary definition of cultural literacy, with the former referring to someone's literacy of their own culture; a culture that is understood as singular and one that exists within national boundaries. The contemporary conceptualization of cultural literacy refers to literacy over a compilation of cultures, an understanding of someone's own identities and their multiplicity, coexisting with and being exposed to other identities and cultural practices. Cultural literacy can therefore be understood as one's ability to put their own cultural affiliation in a global context, including both inherited cultures (through identities of ethnicity, race, religion etc.), as well as acquired ones (through assumed practices, affiliations, and transformational experiences). Johnson (2014) argues that cultural literacy is key in measuring cosmopolitanism, as it is a concept that was initially introduced to enhance nationalism – through mono-cultural literacy – and evolved to acknowledge someone's ability to be literate for multiple cultures.

Undoubtedly, travel is an act that can enhance cultural literacy, yet travelling does not automatically translate into a better understanding of other cultures. Differentiating between emancipatory and harmful tourist encounters, authentic and superficial ones, consensual and unethical ones, can determine the quality of the tourist encounter and its ability to provide accurate insight to a new culture. Johnson (2014) links cultural literacy with cosmopolitan capital, which refers to the ability to acquire comprehensive and realistic representations of other cultures and accordingly shape informed worldviews. Using cultural literacy to measure cosmopolitan capital, cosmopolitanism becomes a tangible and measurable indicator for assessing the contribution of tourist activity to respectful, ethical, and equal intercultural relations globally. Cosmopolitan tourist activity can be identified and differentiated from forms of travel that fail to acknowledge, respect, and empower other communities and cultures in their contemporary authenticity.

Revisiting Figure 1.1 from this perspective, there is an evident divergence in the way one end of the tourist typology spectrum conducts tourism in comparison to the other end. Psychocentric and organized mass tourists prioritize personal comfort and deviate from opportunities of organic interaction with local populations in the destination they are visiting, indicating a preference for tourist zones and staged experiences. This form of engagement is superficial in nature and has little capacity to endorse the visitor's cultural literacy, since there is minimal engagement with authentic forms of local contemporary cultural expression. On the other hand, drifters and allocentric visitors representing the opposite extreme of tourist typologies prioritize this kind of organic engagement with locals and are thus more prone to increase their cultural literacy in reference to the host population, while avoiding tourist zones and other

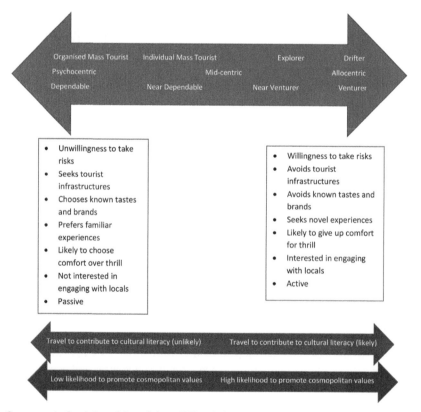

Source: Author (adapted from Cohen, 1972 and Plog, 1974).

Figure 1.2   *Tourist typologies, cosmopolitanism, and international development*

staged settings. Through this observation, it is safe for the tourist typology spectrum offered in Figure 1.1 to serve as an indicator of tourist typologies more prone to increasing their cultural literacy through travel, and as such show increased likelihood for spreading cosmopolitan values and engaging in critical cosmopolitanism through their travels – as illustrated in Figure 1.2.

TOURISM AS A DRIVER FOR INTERNATIONAL DEVELOPMENT

Through cosmopolitan values, we can redefine and refine tourist activity as a political act that is more anthropocentric and less place oriented. According to Carbone (2020), the anthropocentric character of tourism is only expected to grow within the post-pandemic era, putting more emphasis on intercultural dialogue, peace, and development. Carbone (ibid.) highlights the opportunity that the pandemic brought to the tourism industry to restart in a post-pandemic era as a vehicle for human development, and accordingly embrace values of critical cosmopolitanism. Carbone's projection reaffirms the centrality of cosmopolitan values in the future of international tourist activity and endorses the critical aspects of cosmopolitanism that seek to foster emancipation and equality – aspects that will be pursued in the post-pandemic era more intentionally and not merely coincidentally.

To this end, the human-centred approach of tourism and its global contribution through cosmopolitan values can be directly applicable to the pursuit of international development. Through Alkire's (2010) human development definition, development is assessed through its ability to enhance (1) well-being, (2) agency, and (3) justice on a global scale; objectives directly incorporated in critical cosmopolitanism. To pursue critical cosmopolitanism through tourism is, therefore, a pursuit of human development and a priority for post-pandemic tourism development.

It is important to differentiate the anthropocentric character of tourism in reference to human development from forms of anthropocentric tourism that disregard ecosystem and non-human needs. Tourism studies addressing sustainability have identified a need for post-anthropocentric theorizing in examining tourist activity and motivation (Valtonen et al., 2020). Flower et al. (2021) challenge the notion of an anthropocentric worldview with an eco-centric one, through which the former views animals, habitats, and ecosystems in reference to their use for humans. In the context of this book, the anthropocentric character of tourism is established as the priority tourist activities give to interpersonal relations and does not imply a disregard to a destination's non-human inhabitants and ecosystems.

International tourist activity is therefore a catalyst in international development and in the implementation of emancipation and agency through the reduction of inequality and dependency. It is vital to prioritize forms of tourism that endorse cosmopolitan-oriented tourist typologies and promote opportunities for acquiring cultural literacy on a multicultural scale.

Nevertheless, discussions on cosmopolitan worldviews and international development cannot be comprehensive if attention is paid only to the human factor. As Valtonen et al. (2020) and Flower et al. (2021) admit, the examination of tourism and its contribution to development should be post-anthropocentric, considering the world's fauna and ecosystems. While tourism has been projected to adopt more anthropocentric trends to attend to what Todaro and Smith (2009) define as development, contemporary definitions of development have adopted post-anthropocentric perspectives to address not only socio-economic components of development, but also ecological ones. Revisiting the ways in which we understand development from post-anthropocentric perspectives implies a reconstruction of development as a comprehensively sustainable practice.

Sharpley (2020) sees the notion of sustainable development as an oxymoron, a problematic pursuit that is characterized by terminological ambiguity and is comprised of contradictory goals. Robert et al. (2005: 9) admit that there is a malleability to the definition of sustainable development as development that "meets the needs of the present without compromising the ability of future generations to meet their own needs". This definition emphasizes sustainability as a form of intergenerational equity (ibid.), with the authors differentiating between what is to be sustained – the environment, nature, ecosystems, diversity, community, and culture – and what is to be developed – societies, economies, and people's standard of living.

To develop sustainably is a quest that expands the economic-oriented scope of development to acknowledge and consider additional factors of life, resources, and opportunities across communities and generations. Johnsen et al. (2017) visually portray sustainability as three circles consecutively larger, with the economy being the smallest, human societies representing the second circle that fully encompasses the economic one, and the Earth's life support system – the environment and its ecosystems – being illustrated as the largest circle, fully incorporating human societies and their economies. Engelmann et al. (2019) extend the understanding of sustainable development by illustrating how the UN's Sustainable Development Goals address development through six areas: (1) economic added value, (2) environmental protection, (3) social equity, (4) eco-innovation, (5) resource efficiency, and (6) low carbon.

To make sustainable development tangible, measurable, and attainable, the United Nations issued the framework of the Sustainable Development Goals, a set of 17 goals consisting of a total of 169 targets (United Nations, 2022). The goals outline the desired status to be achieved for 17 thematic areas in a manner of intergenerational equity, addressing, among others, poverty, inequality, and economic growth, and additionally education, gender equality, sanitation, innovation, peace, responsible consumption and production, life on land and under water (ibid.).

The Sustainable Development Goals provide a measurable framework for sustainable development that make it a tangible roadmap and end goal. To this end, to discuss tourism as a contributor to development today requires examining which forms of tourist activity can contribute to sustainable development through these elaborate 17 thematic areas. Sharpley (2020) discusses tourism's capacity as an industrial activity; one that may contribute economically to a destination, but is otherwise confined from contributing to sustainable growth and social equity. Revisiting tourism from the perspective of critical cosmopolitanism allows us to re-evaluate this position and reconsider tourism's input to development through its contribution to ecological awareness, community emancipation, and local agency.

The 17 goals can therefore be used as a reference point for evaluating tourism's contribution to each one separately and thus to international development collectively. Forms of tourist activity that follow the drifter/allocentric/venturer tourist typologies are characterized by high likelihood to promote cosmopolitan values and apply them in a critical manner to foster local agency and emancipation. These forms of tourist activity require little to no tourist infrastructure and are easily adaptable to foreign landscapes, cultures, and dynamics. They are not likely to generate negative interactions with locals as the increased cultural literacy of the tourists performing them allows them to address host communities with respect and reciprocity. Such forms of tourist activity can therefore effectively address the 17 goals through niche tourist experiences that meet their specializations, interests, and areas through which they can contribute to the destination, as illustrated in Table 1.1.

The niche tourist activities included in Table 1.1 have been identified through extant scholarship as activities that can contribute positively to one or more aspects of sustainable development across destinations, in ways that acknowledge and respect host input and agency. Responsible tourism is a conscious social act and incorporates actions that make tourism more sustainable (Goodwin, 2022). Ecotourism is a form of responsible tourism to areas of nature and environmental conservation (Ruhanen and Axelsen, 2022), while slow travel is also seen as an environmentally sustainable form of travel that avoids air transportation and instead utilizes slower and more environmentally friendly means of transport (Dickinson, 2022). Inclusive tourism enables marginalized groups to engage in the "ethical production or consumption of tourism and the sharing of its benefits" (Scheyvens and Biddulph, 2018: 592), while social tourism refers to the ability of economically disadvantaged individuals and families to engage in tourism through external support (McGrath, 2022). The emancipatory character of inclusive

Table 1.1   Tourism and sustainable development

Sustainable Development Goal	Niche Tourist Activity (for drifter/allocentric/ venturer visitors with increased cultural literacy)
Goal 1: No Poverty	**Inclusive Tourism, Community-based Tourism**
Goal 2: Zero Hunger	**Inclusive Tourism, Community-based Tourism**
Goal 3: Good Health and Well-being	**Social Tourism, Holistic Tourism, Health Tourism, Inclusive Tourism, Community-based Tourism**
Goal 4: Quality Education	**Voluntourism, Educational Tourism, Social Tourism**
Goal 5: Gender Equality	**Inclusive Tourism, Community-based Tourism, Social Tourism, Peacebuilding Tourism, Language Tourism**
Goal 6: Clean Water and Sanitation	**Responsible Tourism, Slow Travel, Voluntourism**
Goal 7: Affordable and Clean Energy	**Responsible Tourism, Slow Travel, Voluntourism**
Goal 8: Decent Work and Economic Growth	**Inclusive Tourism, Community-based Tourism, Social Tourism**
Goal 9: Industry, Innovation, and Infrastructure	**Inclusive Tourism, Community-based Tourism, Social Tourism**
Goal 10: Reduced Inequality	**Inclusive Tourism, Community-based Tourism, Social Tourism, Language Tourism**
Goal 11: Sustainable Cities and Communities	**Responsible Tourism, Slow Tourism**
Goal 12: Responsible Consumption and Production	**Inclusive Tourism, Community-based Tourism**
Goal 13: Climate Action	**Responsible Tourism, Ecotourism, Slow Travel, Voluntourism**
Goal 14: Life Below Water	**Ecotourism, Slow Travel, Voluntourism**
Goal 15: Life on Land	**Ecotourism, Slow Travel, Voluntourism**
Goal 16: Peace and Justice Strong Institutions	**Peace Tourism, Peacebuilding Tourism**
Goal 17: Partnerships to Achieve the Goals	**Inclusive Tourism, Community-based Tourism, Peacebuilding Tourism**

Source: Author (terms adapted from the *Encyclopedia of Tourism Management and Marketing*, 2022).

tourism is also reflected in community-based tourism, which according to Kepher-Gona and Atieno (2022) ensures community ownership of tourist initiatives and thus directly benefits the host community. Alongside the more known voluntourism and educational tourism, language tourism is a sub-form of educational tourism that is characterized by language learning as a principal tourist activity in the destination visited (Iglesias, 2022). Respectively, holistic tourism is a sub-form of health tourism that incorporates a holistic philosophy towards wellness, spirituality, and well-being (Rahmani and Carr, 2022). Peace tourism is characterized by the traveller's motivation to learn about a destination's roadmap to peace and potentially contribute to it (Antoniou, 2022a). Peacebuilding tourism is a form of peace tourism undertaken by peace professionals and therefore more actively engages with conflict resolution initiatives (Antoniou, 2022b).

These niche tourist activities alone do not guarantee a positive impact on the destination. It is vital that these tourist activities are undertaken by visitors embracing the characteristics of the drifter/allocentric/venturer tourist typologies, who engage with local communities and infrastructure in a way that is likely to be more sustainable, respectful, and ethical than tourist behaviours towards the mass tourism end of the spectrum (see Figure 1.2). These tourists are also more likely to embrace cosmopolitan values and assist rather than dictate to the local population how to progress.

Culturally literate and cosmopolitan tourists can directly promote international development sustainably through tourism. Appropriate niche tourist activities as the ones identified here allow the cosmopolitan and culturally literate tourist to enter a destination's society and greater ecosystem without disrupting it. More importantly, this tourist can engage constructively with the locals and, by providing tools, best practices, and cross-cultural insights to the host population, to allow for conducive and organic interactions to positively inform local practices. Tourism's contribution towards the SDGs is not necessarily one-sided but can have mutual benefits towards both the host community and the visitors themselves. Table 1.2 illustrates each example of niche tourist activity and its potential to contribute to sustainable development through specific goals.

Social tourism directly reduces inequalities by providing travel opportunities to those who cannot afford it. Tourism, therefore, becomes an experience for all and not only for financially established travellers, enabling people from across financial capacities to engage in the benefits of cross-cultural awareness and cultural literacy that tourism offers. In a similar manner, inclusive and community-based tourism enables everyone to be a potential host without commodifying their lifestyle, personal struggles, or themselves. These forms of tourism, when delivered responsibly, can contribute to local agency, and foster locally generated growth and prosperity, while ensuring social equity.

Voluntourism has been criticized for its contribution to social equity due to the risk of creating relationships of dependency across wealthy visitors and developing communities. At the same time, voluntourism can offer significant assistance to initiatives of environmental conservation, alongside forms of ecotourism, responsible tourism, and slow travel.

Holistic and language tourism engage travellers directly with aspects of local culture, practices, rituals and heritage, giving them an insight to the local community through meaningful experiences, and thus contributing to their cultural literacy. From an analogous perspective, travellers engaging in peace and

Table 1.2   *Niche tourism and the SDGs*

Niche Tourist Activity	Sustainable Development Goals Addressed
Community-based Tourism	1, 2, 3, 5, 8, 9, 10, 12, 17
Ecotourism	13, 14, 15
Educational Tourism	4
Health Tourism	3
Holistic Tourism	3
Inclusive Tourism	1, 2, 3, 5, 8, 9, 10, 12, 17
Language Tourism	5, 10
Peace Tourism	16
Peacebuilding Tourism	5, 16, 17
Responsible Tourism	6, 7, 11, 13
Slow Travel	6, 7, 13, 14, 15
Social Tourism	3, 4, 5, 8, 9, 10
Voluntourism	4, 6, 7, 13, 14, 15

Source: Author.

peacebuilding tourism are directly interested in a destination's prospects for peace and stability, and can both increase their own cultural literacy, and at the same time contribute to the destination's peace, stability, equity, and growth.

CONCLUSION

Today, more than ever, tourism can be conceptualized as a conscious and informed political act of international magnitude. The nature of international tourist activity is no longer considered a symptom of the globalized world stage, but it is a driver in international development, shaping relations and input across the world's developed and developing communities. Redefining tourism from the perspective of international development implies the deconstruction of an activity that was considered passive and understanding it as a purposeful act with political intention and socio-political consequences.

There are two significant issues in international tourist activity that this chapter identifies for their direct contribution to transnational relationships of oppression and inequality. The first issue is the depoliticization of politically charged forms of tourism, such as slum and volunteer tourism. The second issue is the distorted views of authenticity that often refer to the non-urbanized and underdeveloped versions of hosting communities, linking authenticity to the host community's struggle for economic independence, empowerment, and self-reliance. Tourist activity undoubtedly carries ethical responsibilities, and its often-overlooked impact on the political, economic, and social status of developing and disadvantaged communities can lead to negative contributions to international development.

An effective way of addressing this phenomenon is to first differentiate across forms of tourism with a higher and lower likelihood to have negative encounters with the host communities of visited destinations. Using the parameters of cultural literacy and cosmopolitanism there is a clear distinction between organized mass forms of tourism, which tend to be more passive, less informed, and less sustainable, and forms of tourism that embrace responsible travel and engage with host communities in more organic and respectful ways.

To measure tourism's contribution to development, the chapter employs a tourism typology spectrum and identifies forms of tourism that can apply critical cosmopolitanism and hence positively and sustainably contribute to a destination's human, societal, economic, and ecological development. These forms of tourism can make direct contributions to the development areas outlined by the UN's Sustainable Development Goals, which provide a measurable output for progress on sustainable development internationally. Tourism can contribute to social, environmental, and economic sustainability through forms of tourist activity that entail critical applications of cosmopolitanism. Tourism is, therefore, much more than an industrial activity, as argued by Sharpley (2020), and can be considered an impactful socioeconomic, environmental, ethical, and political act.

2. Tourism and diplomacy

INTRODUCTION

The practice of modern diplomacy has been referred to as the "official nego-tiations between representatives of states" (Baranowski et al., 2019: 63). It finds its roots in the seventeenth century and the Treaty of Westphalia, which followed a process of "official negotiations between representatives of states" to create the modern state as we know it. It is therefore not surprising that diplomacy has developed with a state-centric character, focusing on the dia-logue and relations performed between states.

In recent decades, however, the international political stage has witnessed an evident shift in diplomatic discourse expanding beyond its state-centric character, making diplomacy – in line with international relations more broadly – a practice of negotiation involving both state representatives and other non-state actors. The latter have been reported at the forefront of interna-tional affairs with mounting frequency. Echoing this phenomenon, the practice of diplomacy has evolved to incorporate diplomatic activity that includes a wide range of non-state entities, including civil society organizations, non-governmental institutions, and individuals.

Public diplomacy has been a dominant example of what scholarship has referred to as new diplomacy. As a state-led activity, public diplomacy aims to directly engage with public opinion. More broadly, it has also been described as an instrument of both state and non-state actors to understand cultures, shape relationships, and generate political action (Melissen, 2013). According to Gilboa (2008), the rationale behind public diplomacy was to sway public opinion in support of state policies and foreign policy agendas, and to estab-lish a positive public profile for a nation abroad. Ang et al. (2015) discuss the example of cultural diplomacy as one of many branches of contemporary public diplomacy. The authors suggest that defining cultural diplomacy solely as a state-centric practice designed to endorse national interests is an obsolete approach that prevents discussions on diplomatic activity from moving beyond the state sphere. Instead, differentiating the act of cultural *diplomacy*, which is government-led, from cultural *relations*, which is organically driven by ideals that transcend beyond national boundaries, may provide a more comprehen-sive understanding of contemporary diplomatic discourse (ibid.).

The evolution of diplomacy challenges the state-centric nature of diplomacy and poses the question: is the term *diplomacy* one that is reserved for state-led encounters? If not, and if the term can expand to incorporate political actors beyond the state, is diplomacy then solely about state interests? In better understanding diplomacy in a post-state international political stage, it is important to specify whether international diplomacy is discussed with reference solely to the national interests of states, or whether the interests of non-state actors should also be incorporated into a broader spectrum of postmodern international diplomatic discourse.

This chapter employs the perspective of tourism to examine whether contemporary diplomacy remains invested in advancing state interests through a broader network of state and non-state actors, or whether we have moved to an era of *post-state*, or *cosmopolitan diplomacy* that is characterized by communication across a diversity of international political actors to address global causes. In doing so, the political impact of international tourist activity is revealed both in relation to state interests and causes transcending state boundaries.

A REVIEW OF MODERN DIPLOMACY

In his 1994 account on *Diplomacy*, Henry Kissinger presents the United States as the twentieth-century's leading political actor, a beacon of democracy, and a model of "intellectual and moral impetus" (Kissinger, 1994: 17). At the dawn of the post-Cold War era, Kissinger praises the role of the United States as a world leader tasked with crafting a new world order according to the values of democracy and state sovereignty.

While diplomacy has evolved to represent the formal and protocolled dialogue that occurs between official representatives of states, it finds its roots in epochs prior to the existence of the modern Westphalian state. Cohen (2013) discusses interactions between sovereigns from the ancient Mesopotamian era, which marks the emergence of urban civilizations. What is referred to as classical diplomacy was also recorded during the rule of the Persian Empire and in reference to dialogue with ancient Greece (ibid.). Cohen (2013) additionally identifies Roman diplomacy as the communicative approach of the Roman empire, which was based on dominance and not on reciprocal exchange among equals. With the creation of the modern sovereign state being marked in 1648 by the Treaty of Westphalia, forms of European diplomacy were recorded prior to this date, particularly in the Renaissance period of the fifteenth century, and the Middle Ages (1200–1500) (ibid.). In the early twentieth century, scholars engaged with the study of diplomacy as a means for understanding international relations, which at the time was defined as the relationships between nation-states (Pigman, 2013).

Undoubtedly, the evolution of diplomacy from archaic periods to today assumed a variety of shapes and forms, from the exchange of letters and gifts to personal relations among kings, and from coerced allegiance to dialogue in the pursuit of understanding other actors of the international political stage. Kerr and Wiseman (2013: 1) refer to the evolution and diversity of diplomatic discourse as the "diplomacy puzzle"; in its contemporary form, it engages both state and non-state actors, and formulates around the key global themes that drive international relations, including the environment, and the global economy.

Environmental diplomacy came into use with the creation of the United Nations Environment Programme (UNEP) in 1973, which provided a structure for negotiation and coordinated action on environmental conservation (Ali and Vladich, 2016). It is a practice that enables global environmental governance to be negotiated and agreed upon, primarily among state actors that commit to achieving environmental sustainability within their sovereign territory (ibid.). Key international agreements on environmental sustainability have been supported and implemented by nation-states in the past decades through UNEP, an achievement that is recorded as Track One diplomacy, while non-state actors engaging in transnational environmental action are considered Track Two diplomacy.

Woolcock (2013) refers to economic diplomacy as a form of negotiation that shapes international economic realities and determines the course of key international economic activities such as trade, investment, and finance. The definition of diplomacy as a form of negotiation between international political actors (Baranowski et al., 2019) is also endorsed by Zartman (2013), who highlights that globalization has expanded international processes of negotiation to aim not only for state security, but also for human security on an individual level, and international security on a systemic level. In a similar vein, one can argue that diplomacy has expanded to be not only guided by national interest but also informed and shaped by individual and transnational concerns.

The expansive nature of contemporary diplomacy has yielded frequent exchanges not only among state actors, but also across state and non-state actors, a practice that has been referred to as polylateral diplomacy. According to Spies (2019), polylateral diplomacy is a networked model intersecting statecraft with civilcraft, or representatives of state actors with the non-state actors representing organized civil society. Gregory (2016) states that polylateral diplomacy engages non-state actors through standard diplomatic practice that incorporates communication, representation, and negotiation. Defining polylateral diplomacy through the blurry lines separating state diplomacy from the activity of their non-state political counterparts is a complex task that challenges the essence of modern diplomacy as the art of negotiation between state officials. Gregory (2016: 1) distinguishes between "governance actors" engaging in diplomacy and civil society practising cosmopolitanism. From a critical angle analogous to Gregory's, Spies (2019: 153) argues that non-state actors engage in de facto diplomacy; acknowledging, nonetheless, their role as diplomatic actors, Spies suggests that contemporary diplomacy takes place at a "global public commons", where state and societal interests intersect. The United Nations Security Council has created an informal space for polylateral diplomacy to occur, which provides UNSC members with the capacity to engage with non-members and civil society actors through private meetings. This exchange has been referred to as the Arria Formula (Wiseman and Basu, 2013).

The evolution of modern diplomacy to incorporate stakeholders beyond the state actor led to the emergence of public diplomacy, which is characterized by direct communication of state actors with the public. State-led public diplomacy that was used as a tool for promoting foreign policy agendas to the public was criticized as a form of propaganda rather than a genuine form of dialogue between states and people (Melissen, 2013). Nevertheless, state governments are not the only actors employing public diplomacy, with both corporate and non-governmental organizations utilizing this tool to engage in diplomatic dialogue with the public and shape public policy (ibid.). It is possible for governments and civil society – or other non-state actors – to align their engagement with public diplomacy and reinforce a common message transnationally, or to differentiate it (ibid.).

Forms of public diplomacy include cultural, educational, sports, heritage, and gastronomic as examples of approaches for engaging in dialogue with foreign citizens. The US Fulbright programme for university students and academics, as well as the British Council's work in language and university education, offer examples of educational diplomacy that have been used for decades to engage foreign nationals with the academic institutions in the US and the UK respectively. According to Vaxevanidou (2017), public diplomacy in its various forms has become a tool in nation branding and rebranding in ways that establish a state actor's credibility and global impact among foreign audiences.

The act of diplomacy, and more specifically forms of public diplomacy, provide a striking resemblance to forms of contemporary tourist activity, which in a similar manner brings the public close to foreign states through a variety of interest-based, culturally informed, educational, or gastronomic activities. To understand the broadening scope of diplomacy as it evolves to incorporate both formal and informal processes, and to engage both state and non-state international stakeholders, the angle of tourism gives appropriate insight to the transnational exchange of ideas and nonformal, interest-based, and culturally informed communication.

Public diplomacy has developed to act as an umbrella term that encompasses forms of state-oriented diplomacy that is not performed exclusively by state actors and their representatives. Payne et al. (2011) introduce the concept of grassroots public diplomacy, which can assume different meanings when examined from two diverging perspectives: the realist and the liberalist one. Through the realist perspective, grassroots public diplomacy is an activity directed by a state government to advance its interests, making it synonymous with public diplomacy. From a liberalist perspective, which assumes that the state actor is not the principal one in diplomatic affairs, but merely one of many actors on the international political stage, grassroots public diplomacy is the long-term initiative for dialogue and understanding across these actors (ibid.). Payne (2009: 487) explains grassroots public diplomacy as the means through which both "nongovernmental organizations and individual voices" active at the grassroots level engage in diplomatic affairs with one another to address global issues that traditional state diplomacy has failed to attend to.

Although state actors remain central to international diplomatic discourse, the communication and coordinated political action between non-state actors has been incorporated into the diplomacy puzzle and the widening scope of contemporary diplomacy. Track Two diplomacy has been employed as a term that refers to dialogue across civil society actors, non-governmental organizations, and institutions within and across sovereign states that do not operate on a governmental level, or Track One, and therefore conduct diplomatic dialogue independently of state positions and interests (Kerr and Taylor, 2013). This form of new diplomacy is one that deviates from focusing on national foreign policy and one that engages with transnational topics and areas of global concern (ibid.), establishing discourse for coordinated policymaking towards global – rather than state-specific – goals. One example of Track Two diplomacy is environmental diplomacy undertaken by non-state, civil society actors.

An interesting and emergent form of diplomacy is citizen diplomacy, or *diplomacy of the public*, a form of diplomatic activity that puts the citizen at the forefront of international diplomatic activity. Melisssen (2013) describes citizen diplomacy as the interaction between social collectives with the aim of cultivating a shared meaning and understanding of one another's communities and culture. While the citizen is considered a representative of the state and society that they are a member of, it would be simplistic to assume that they abide by the positions of their state's foreign policy agenda. It is therefore a form of diplomacy performed by the citizen that does not show a clear-cut relationship between citizen and state objectives, and how these may or may not align. According to Tyler and Beyerinck (2016), it remains ambiguous whether citizen diplomacy incorporates components of official state diplomacy, or whether it more broadly refers to individuals engaging in cross-border relations.

Diplomacy in the post-Cold War era has evolved in ways that have taken the practice well beyond its formal state character, a development that Wiseman and Kerr (2013: 339) associate with the phenomenon of globalization and the "information revolution" it has, and continues to, generate. Table 2.1 outlines how contemporary diplomacy can be illustrated through six forms, indicating the stakeholders engaged in each one.

Table 2.1   Forms of contemporary diplomacy

ACTORS	States	States and Non-state actors	States and People	Non-state actors	Non-state actors and People	People
Forms of diplomacy	Modern diplomacy	Polylateral diplomacy	Public diplomacy	Track Two diplomacy	Grassroots diplomacy	Citizen diplomacy
	State diplomacy			Civil society diplomacy		

Source: Author.

A profound realization that comes from Table 2.1 is that, although discussions of modern diplomacy encompass contemporary diplomacy in all its forms, international diplomatic activity extends well beyond the definition of modern diplomacy as an exchange of ideas and positions between formal representatives of states. While Table 2.1 illustrates forms of diplomacy as distinct categories based on the stakeholders that perform them, many of these terms intersect, illustrating unclear boundaries as to where one form of diplomacy ends and the other one begins. What Table 2.1 highlights is that, despite the vagueness around the categorization of diplomatic activity, there is a distinct differentiation between diplomacy that is implemented by or directly engages state actors, and diplomacy undertaken by civil society actors, whether these are grassroots organizations, individual citizens, or both. In contemporary international relations, and to this end in contemporary diplomacy, these two categories of actors – state and non-state – do not carry out their international activity in isolation of one another. To the contrary, the steady emergence of non-state actors as diplomatic agents enables more and more avenues of diplomatic communication across state and non-state diplomats, further blurring the lines that differentiate between diplomacy for state interests and diplomacy for global causes. The engagement of diplomacy actors through tourism is no exception to this phenomenon, as diplomacy through tourism can equally address state and global objectives and engage the multitude of stakeholders that perform contemporary diplomacy.

PRACTISING DIPLOMACY THROUGH TOURISM

Short-term travel is essential for diplomatic exchange. Where it involves state actors, their representatives engage in visitation to foreign territories to conduct diplomatic dialogue in person. In the case of non-state actors, individual professionals and activists, representatives of civil society organizations, and members of global networks and institutions utilize tourism to conduct diplomatic relations and join global initiatives for political action.

When examining the relationship between tourism and diplomacy, the most usual form of diplomacy discussed is public diplomacy. For example, scholarship has considered the reciprocal relationship between public diplomacy and tourism advertising. The latter is seen as a tool for enhancing public diplomacy and improving a nation's image among foreign audiences (Fullerton and Kendrick, 2013) while public diplomacy expands beyond foreign policy objectives to incorporate the objective of increased tourist inflows (Gu et al., 2022). Public diplomacy has also been discussed interchangeably with citizen diplomacy, in cases where citizens are viewed as representatives of their states when interacting with foreign audiences. This is frequently observed in international tourist activity and in the interactions of tourist audiences with host populations. In this example of transnational exchange, citizen diplomacy is viewed as a form of public diplomacy through which tourists introduce host communities to their individual habits and attitudes, which are then assumed as representative behaviours of their culture and nationality. Public diplomacy in the case of tourism may occur without the tourist intentionally promoting a positive image of their affiliated state. In the case of rude or hostile attitudes a negative image of the state emerges, reinforcing stereotypes and prejudice.

Another example of tourism's direct association with diplomacy is tourist activities that provide the platform and conditions for individuals – whether as representatives of a community, a social group, an organization, or in their personal capacity – to engage in negotiations, communication and idea exchange, activism, or other forms of political activity during their short-term travel and within their capacity as tourists. These activities could be defined as *tourism-led* or *tourism-performed diplomacy*.

Experts joining international policy fora such as UN, EU, and G7 summits contribute to negotiations in their professional capacity and not as representatives of states. Policy summits of this nature also attract participation by individual activists, protesters, and civil society organizations, who provide their input to the official agenda discussed. Their capacity as tourists provides them with access to the discussion being held, enabling them to make their political contribution. An analogous example of civil society diplomacy can be identified in the work of think tanks and lobby groups, which incorporates advocacy directed at supranational entities, but also by sharing their message with the public through transnational marches, protests, and illustrations. In addition to the examples of expert policy contributions, transnational activism, and advocacy, tourism-led diplomacy can also be traced in non-state summits, conferences, and professional forums, which provide the platform and network for professionals of specific sectors to identify global challenges in their area of expertise and address these through dialogue, idea exchange, and coordinated action. Peacebuilding practitioners, medical experts, researchers, and engineers are only a few examples of practitioners informing their work through international best practice exchange that occurs by joining professional summits and conferences as short-term travellers, while also negotiating through their input the international practice to be followed in that area of work. The diversity of tourism-led diplomacy is as broad as the scope of tourist activity that is non-passive and thus achieves a level of socio-political impact. Diplomacy through tourism can, therefore, take place through a diversity of experiential forms of tourism that incorporate the negotiated exchange of ideas across international political actors – including individual citizens. This activity can be further refined by differentiating between tourism-led diplomacy oriented towards state interests, and tourism-led diplomacy led by transnational, cosmopolitan values.

State Diplomacy and Tourism

Baranowski et al. (2019) present tourism as an actor in state diplomacy, and tourists as representatives of their states abroad. Leisure tourists represent their respective states and governments through nonformal political discussions they have while travelling. Other times, tourism diplomacy is about avoiding politics, and showing the willingness to connect and build bridges with historically rival political entities, or controversial states, such as post-World War II Germany (ibid.). Through their travels, tourists become public diplomats that take on mediator and translator roles between the states and cultures they represent. In accordance with what Baranowski et al. discuss, international tourist activity should be seen as a vehicle for improved relations among states, since interpreting other cultures and their dynamics provides the ground for transnational empathy and understanding.

Bunakov et al. (2018) agree with the notion that tourists act as representatives of their states abroad, and call tourism a tool of soft power in modern diplomacy. This approach encompasses the entrenched connection states hold with the concept of diplomacy: even when scholarship discusses interactions and relations between individuals that have no formal affiliation with the state that they are citizens of – which in cases of dual citizenship can be more than one – there interactions are assumed to serve the state. Scholarly discussions of diplomacy conducted by non-state actors are often conducted in reference to the impact and benefits delivered to state actors.

Noack (in Baranowski et al., 2019) identifies the parallels between the state diplomat and the tourist. They both engage in transnational mobility, to encounter foreign cultures and attempt to make sense of them, with the diplomat reporting their experiences back to the government, for purposes of policymaking, while the tourist reports their engagement with the destination to peers in the form of recollection or travel advice. What Noack suggests here is that state diplomats become coincidental tourists for their work objectives, while tourists may become coincidental diplomats by shaping the opinions of their peers regarding the destination and host community they visited. A key realization offered by Baranowski et al. (2019) is that there can be different forms of state sovereignty, and there can be various impacts derived from tourist activity, moving the discussion beyond a straightforward relationship between tourism and state diplomacy.

Cosmopolitan Diplomacy and Tourism

The alternative to state diplomacy that has been detected through the gradual emergence of non-state diplomatic actors has been non-state, or civil society diplomacy, in reference to the actors conducting it. According to Anton (2022), civil society diplomacy (CSD) can be used as an umbrella term for the forms of diplomacy conducted by civil society and non-state actors of the international political stage. This term can be difficult to disengage from state diplomacy, as there is a notable tendency among scholarly discussions of diplomacy to formulate their analysis in relation to state interests, regardless of whether the actors involved are states or non-state agents. Ang et al. (2015) suggest, in reference to cultural diplomacy, that diplomacy conducted by non-state actors that advances the interests of non-state entities and global movements is not considered diplomacy, but merely another example of international relations. Yet to overlook the diplomatic nature of this niche form of international relations, with the negotiating and coordinating character it entails, would be an oversight to the field of International Relations altogether.

An attempt to redefine contemporary diplomacy should therefore take into consideration not only the actors involved in diplomatic activity, but also the interests served. Extant literature suggests a principal interest-based differentiation: diplomacy for state interests, and diplomacy for non-state or global interests. The latter is defined here as *cosmopolitan diplomacy*, aiming to acknowledge the cosmopolitan philosophy behind globally beneficial end goals, as well as the diverse nature of the actors pursuing them. Gulmez introduced the term cosmopolitan diplomacy in 2018 to emphasize the type of diplomacy that is driven by interests transcending national boundaries.

Gulmez (2018), however, spoke of cosmopolitan diplomacy as an activity performed exclusively by states, a definition that is more confined than the one employed here, as illustrated in Table 2.2.

Table 2.2   *Actors in contemporary diplomacy*

ACTORS	States	States and Non-state actors	States and People	Non-state actors	Non-state actors and People	People
Forms of diplomacy	Modern diplomacy	Polylateral diplomacy	Public diplomacy	Track Two diplomacy	Grassroots diplomacy	Citizen diplomacy
		State diplomacy		Civil society diplomacy		
Likely to advance state interests (State-oriented diplomacy)	✓	✓	✓	✓	✓	✓
Likely to advance global interests (Cosmopolitan diplomacy)	✓	✓	✓	✓	✓	✓

Source: Author.

Differentiating between state-oriented and cosmopolitan diplomacy based on the interests it addresses and not by exclusively defining the actors performing it enables the hybridity and interconnectedness of international actors in diplomacy to be acknowledged and to be more accurately represented. Additionally, this conceptualization of contemporary diplomacy allows for a more accurate understanding of the role of tourism in each of these two categories of diplomatic discourse, whether intentional or coincidental. Figure 2.1 illustrates forms of contemporary diplomacy conducted through tourism in four main categories.

Figure 2.1 provides an illustration of how a discussion of tourism and diplomacy can be more rounded when taking into consideration diplomatic activity conducted both for state and non-state objectives, as well as diplomacy conducted both intentionally and coincidentally. The four categories of diplomatic discourse identified in this figure are the four principal ways in which tourism becomes a means to conduct diplomacy: (1) by intentionally using tourism to enhance state interests; (2) by doing so coincidentally; (3) by employing tourism intentionally to advance global interests; and (4) by serving global interests through tourism-led diplomacy coincidentally. To comprehend

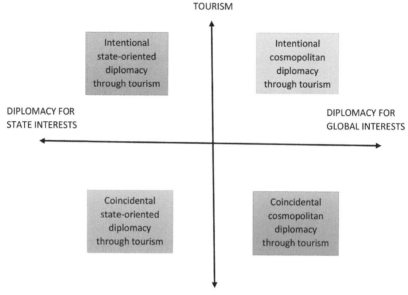

Source: Author.

Figure 2.1   Tourism and diplomacy

tourism's role and contribution in contemporary diplomacy, Figure 2.1 is discussed further using the IR field's Levels of Analysis approach – an approach introduced and explained in detail in the following section.

TOURISM AND THE IR LEVELS OF ANALYSIS

International political activity can be analysed at an individual, a state, or a systemic level (Rourke and Boyer, 2008; Mingst et al., 2018). Each level of analysis offers a distinct angle from which international relations discourse – and in this context, diplomacy – is examined, analysed, and evaluated. The individual level observes the weight that individual initiative and decision-making carries, and what socio-political impact it generates more broadly. The state level offers a state-centric narrative of international political discourse, acknowledging state actors as the protagonists. State-level analyses are primarily concerned with the ways in which state actors affect and are affected by international relations. The third level of analysis is concerned with the international system as a whole and observes political activity as it occurs between actors that are components of the system as a unit. The systemic level is therefore primarily interested in global phenomena and socio-political activity of transnational dynamic.

In the case of diplomacy, the individual level of analysis offers insights to the decision-making of individual diplomats and actors engaged in the art of diplomacy as negotiation, communication, and idea exchange. The state level focuses its approach on state actors and it, therefore, prioritizes the examination of state diplomacy over forms of civil society and cosmopolitan diplomacy. While the latter is still a category of diplomatic discourse that can be examined and explained through the state level of analysis, such an examination would be conducted to understand the effects of civil society and cosmopolitan forms of diplomacy on state actors. From a contrasting angle, the systemic level's take on diplomatic activity would not necessarily identify the impact this has on individual actors of the international political stage, but instead how the scope of contemporary diplomatic exchange, in its diversity, informs and shapes international political dynamics altogether. As each level of analysis can offer its distinct insights on international diplomacy, the following paragraphs offer an overview of this analytical framework to establish its association with international diplomacy and its applicability to contemporary tourist practice.

Individual Level of Analysis

According to Rourke and Boyer (2008), the individual level of analysis emphasizes the role of an individual leader in shaping the course of history, an approach that emphasizes how international decisions can be affected by a leader's cognitive conditions, emotional influences, and even biological factors. International Relations scholarship has employed the individual level of analysis to examine the impact of influential leaders such as Mikhael Gorbachev (Miller, 1991; Lane, 1996; Shakibi, 2010) and Nelson Mandela (Adam and Moodley, 2005; Lodge, 2007; Boehmer, 2008). More broadly, the individual IR analytical approach also incorporates the role of individual agents within organizations, and how groupthink, role behaviour, and one's position within a broader institutional entity affects their decision-making and profile as individuals.

The individual level of analysis should not only be utilized for acknowledging individual state leaders, or leaders of international political organizations, as then it would risk adopting a state-centric approach to IR. Individuals within non-state political organizations and entities, as well as individual citizens, activists, and influential figures across state boundaries can also be examined for their role and input in international political discourse. With this understanding in mind, the individual level of analysis becomes applicable to the study of diplomacy through the decision-making of state representatives, non-state actor ambassadors, and individual citizens with a transnational political influence.

Interestingly, it is unclear whether the individual level of analysis can incorporate and assess the political impact of individual organizations and group entities – for example local civil society groups, NGOs with a transnational impact, or international platforms with a global influence such as Facebook and Amazon – who can engage with polylateral diplomacy as internationally influential private entities. Such entities of a non-governmental nature can be considered individual non-state actors with input that directly shapes international political communication. In an analogous example, the Airbnb platform is an undoubtedly catalytic stakeholder in vacation rentals and hospitality accommodation, and it can be identified as an individual stakeholder with global socio-political influence.

With regards to international tourist activity, the individual level of analysis attends directly to the individual tourist and examines decision-making at the individual level that leads to political exchange and negotiation through tourism. Individual travellers act as ambassadors of their cultural, national, and wider ideological affiliations, engaging in forms of public and citizen diplomacy. Their choices, activities, and stance while travelling can endorse or condemn certain political phenomena, directly or otherwise. Political acts that gain momentum through tourist activity provide input to the international political scene, with examples including volunteer tourism to impoverished communities, and peace tourism to conflict zones such as Darfur, Rwanda, and the Palestinian territories, for raising international awareness. Therefore, the contribution of influential individuals to international diplomacy and political discourse can be an enlightening angle when examining the impact of tourism on contemporary diplomacy.

State Level of Analysis

The state-centric analysis of international affairs is an approach employed extensively in the understanding of international affairs, as it accepts the state as the dominant stakeholder in international affairs. This is not surprising, considering the historical evolution of international politics and structures of world order, which have treated the state as the principal political structure through which political exchange has been conducted.

Systems of internal societal order and structures of the international system, otherwise referred to as international or world order, were a point of reference for scholars over the centuries. The formation of autonomous political entities, their societal structures and diplomatic discourse, which were recorded by founding political philosophers Plato and Aristotle in ancient Greece, have directly informed political discourse thereafter, as well as modern political entity formation. The ancient Greek city-state, or *polis*, operated as a self-governing society equivalent to the modern nation state, resembling the Westphalian model of state anarchy.

In 1648, a series of peace treaties were signed to restore peace in Europe and involved Spain, the Roman Empire, France, and the Dutch Republic. The treaties were signed in the cities of Westphalia and are today considered the birth mark of the modern state as they acknowledged the right of a self-governed entity for self-determination or, in other words, the state's right to sovereignty (Gross, 1948; Krasner, 1996). The treaties also established the individual's right to civil and political freedoms as citizens of the state, while states of different religion were to be tolerated and treated equally (ibid.). Although the Peace of Westphalia failed to secure the peaceful coexistence of Europe's societies, it established the modern state and the international political structure of state anarchy, or the coexistence of sovereign states in the absence of a global authority.

State sovereignty has been a key feature of the Westphalian international political structure – which is also known as state anarchy. Gross (1948) claims that the Westphalian model concluded its course as soon as the United Nations was founded, serving as the first supranational entity of global governance, and thus compromising the Westphalian model of state sovereignty. According to Krasner (1996), the Westphalian model had been compromised since its conception, as many entities that are considered sovereign were never self-governed. States have been coerced to accept universal principles that affect their rule of law and self-governance and are not, therefore, autonomous, since they cannot exercise their authority over a designated territory in full capacity. Newman (2009) speaks of state failure and the exercise of international governance as an indication of the transition towards a post-Westphalian world order. Hettne (2002) differentiates international order from world order, claiming that international order refers to the international system of sovereign states – the Westphalian model – while world order, a term increasingly employed over the former, refers to the post-Westphalian model of global governance through international and supranational institutions; a world "beyond national sovereignty" (Hettne, 2002: 8). The debate over the blurry lines of state sovereignty has been one directly informed by modern diplomacy, which has incorporated the multilateral communication across states for negotiating their terms of autonomy in an increasingly interconnected and interdependent world.

The state level of analysis has been applied across a wide variety of IR literature, including single-case study accounts, comparative analyses of states (Bercovitch, 1996; Colin et al., 2007; Lennon and Kozlowski, 2008), foreign policy (Neack, 2008; Butler, 2012) and intergroup conflict (Pandey, 1997; Bishara, 2001; Hannay, 2005; Welt, 2010). Understanding international tourist activity through the state-centric scope appears less popular than the individual level of analysis, since individuals are more prominent actors in tourism than states. Nevertheless, applying the state-centric approach can reveal the role of state actors in supporting, restricting, and shaping international tourist activity through regulations and governance. The COVID-19 pandemic and its impact on international tourism is an example of when the state level of analysis proves insightful in revealing how states applied travel regulations with the aim of limiting the spread of the COVID-19 virus within their territories. Although international collaboration and coordination was evident across state actors through formal diplomatic exchange, each state decided on their own regulations and directly affected travellers leaving from and coming to their sovereign vicinity. The pandemic example and the international reaction of state actors proves that, despite international political activity moving beyond the monopoly of states, a state-centric perspective remains relevant in understanding the correlation between contemporary diplomacy and tourism.

Systemic Level of Analysis

An evident observation when looking at the discourse of political order is that states, despite their acclaimed sovereignty, have not been acting in isolation of one another, whether that implies their allegiance to a regional concord or their adaptation to an international norm. English School scholars identify this observation by referring to the international arena not so much as state anarchy, but more as a society of states (Bull, 1977; Wight, 1977). The interconnectedness of international political actors has enabled many socio-political and economic phenomena to occur across state boundaries, at an international scale, making diplomatic dialogue between political actors more frequent and necessary than ever before.

The continuously changing international environment, the emergence of non-state actors, and the rise of global challenges such as climate change, terrorism, and human rights violations has led to a shift towards the systemic analysis of international relations. While non-state actors are effectively analysed from individual-oriented approaches, there seems to be a growing interest in the systemic analysis of their international political activity, with close attention paid in the literature to the activity of non-state actors in reference to global governance (Holzscheiter, 2005), international security (Buzan and Wæver, 2003), terrorism (Kaldor, 2001), economic development (Easterly, 2002), and globalization (Friedman, 2005). International phenomena that have been centrally featured in the study of contemporary tourism include the Fordism and post-Fordism models of production and consumption, globalization, as well as the concept of Westernization within the West vs the Rest cultural and socioeconomic dichotomy.

To view the world as an interconnected political field of interdependent actors has been rigorously achieved through the notion of Cosmopolitanism, which was initially presented by Immanuel Kant as the philosophy of humans as world citizens. Cheah (2006) refers to Kant as the inaugural figure of cosmopolitanism, a philosophy than was later developed further, to encapsulate the active participation of each world citizen in shaping the world stage. Analogous attention to the individual's role in international political and diplomatic discourse is paid by the notion of a global civil society, which refers to organized civic political activity and communication that transcends state boundaries to attend to global phenomena (Kaldor, 2003, 2020; Keane, 2003). Citizen diplomacy, grassroots diplomacy, and Track Two diplomacy, which can be categorized under the umbrella term civil society diplomacy, refer directly to the communication, negotiation, and coordinated action taken at the global civil society level, to address global phenomena and emerging global crises. It is the diplomatic discourse that is driven by the movements of politically organized individuals across state affiliations to secure individual political interests, ideologies, and agendas collectively. The systemic level of analysis offers direct insight to these interests and provides the angle that can most effectively identify and explain global civil society initiatives, including those pursued through tourist activity.

TOURISM'S ROLE IN CONTEMPORARY DIPLOMACY: A LEVELS OF ANALYSIS APPROACH

State-centrism is not a foreign concept to diplomacy, but more so the conventional approach. Using the state level of analysis to understand the role of tourism in contemporary diplomacy brings state interests to the forefront, posing the question: in what ways does tourism elevate state interests through diplomatic activity? Intentionally, a prominent example is forms of public diplomacy that engage tourists in the promotion of their nation and culture, both through intentional initiatives as well as in indirect and unintentional ways. Nevertheless, public diplomacy does not prevent tourists from engaging with cosmopolitan diplomacy, joining global movements, or working towards challenges of transnational concern. The example of educational tourism through public diplomacy programs such as Fulbright, Erasmus, and the British Council reaffirms that many young scholars travel the world for educational purposes and could represent their state and its image while engaging in work of cosmopolitan interest at the same time.

To this end, employing the state level of analysis to understand the role of tourism in contemporary diplomacy is problematic, as it focuses on only one type of political agent, the state. Likewise, the systemic level offers its analysis in a restricted capacity, not by omitting key political players from its focus, but by failing to clearly differentiate between diplomatic activity that serves cosmopolitan versus state interests. This is a key distinction for examining the input of the individual tourist in contemporary diplomacy, who has the potential to serve either state or cosmopolitan objectives. Instead, employing the individual level of analysis overcomes this challenge, because it shifts the focus from the activity of diplomacy and its aftermath to the actor being examined: the tourist. Examining the relationship between tourism and diplomacy from an individual perspective suggests that the focus of this activity is the tourist, and their motivations, expectations, and objectives when engaging in diplomatic discourse. This realization verifies the individual level of analysis as the most appropriate to be applied in this discussion.

To focus on the tourist and effectively differentiate whether a tourist's engagement with diplomacy is intentional or coincidental, a useful model to be considered is the Push and Pull Factors model that explains the internal and external factors shaping motivation and destination choices when travelling (Dann, 1977). The model, coined by Dann in 1977 and employed heavily in tourism research thereafter, refers to the psychographic characteristics of tourists that internally shape their preferences, priorities, and decision-making – the push factors – while the pull factors are the characteristics offered by a destination meeting those preferences and matching the tourist's internal drivers. The Push and Pull Factors model is employed here to inform the four categories of tourists engaging with diplomacy as illustrated in Figure 2.1 and creates four distinct profiles of contemporary tourist diplomats.

In addition to the Push and Pull Factors model, it is important to further understand the tourist's psychographic incentives from a personality perspective. McCrae and Costa (1985) provide five personality categories that have been employed in tourism to assess tourist motivation and character, and thus further inform the analysis of tourist-performed diplomacy. The Big Five personality model, as it is often referred to, illustrates the personality categories of (1) extraversion, (2) agreeableness, (3) conscientiousness, (4) neuroticism, and (5) openness. The extraverted personality is driven primarily by a desire for social interaction, exploration, and active engagement with new crowds and novel experiences. Agreeableness indicates a similar preference for communal rather than solitary activities, and the ability to adjust personal preferences to go with the flow of the group. The agreeable personality also incorporates high levels of empathy, as well as a willingness to volunteer and support others (Kvasova, 2015). Kvasova (2015) describes the conscientious personality as one that prioritizes organization, order, self-discipline, and responsibility. The neurotic personality, on the other hand, shows little control over stress management, making individuals in this category more emotional and impulsive (Verma et al., 2017). The last of the five personality categories, referred to as openness, or openness to experience, describes personalities that are intellectually curious and culturally literate, are open to new and educational experiences, and show broadmindedness and an aptitude for aesthetics and art (ibid.). The McCrae and Costa personality categories have frequently been applied in Tourism scholarship to examine how tourists engage with leisure tourism and niche forms of tourist activity, such as ecotourism (Kvasova, 2015) and religious tourism (Abbate and Di Nuovo, 2013). The Big Five are employed below to further inform the four categories of tourist diplomats identified in Figure 2.1.

The Intentional State-oriented Diplomat

The intention of this tourist diplomat is to utilize their travels to consciously and methodically advance state interests for a state they represent, either formally or informally. This category includes formal state diplomats that travel to conduct diplomatic negotiations and speak on behalf of their state. Travel opportunities for state diplomats, politicians, and heads of state include examples of international organization forums and summits, such as annual assemblies of the UN, regional EU, AU, and NATO summits, and G7 or G20 meetings.

Intentional state-oriented diplomacy is also likely to be conducted by non-governmental officers who nonetheless engage in international functions and competitions in their national capacity, and thus as representatives of their respective states. Examples of intentional state-oriented tourist diplomats that are not government officials include athletes in regional and international competitions such as the Olympic Games and the World Cup, singers and performers in the Eurovision Song Contest participating on behalf of their country, internationally acclaimed Nobel Laureates, as well as artists, chefs, and actors with international awards and accolades.

The push factors motivating intentional state-oriented diplomats to conduct diplomacy through tourism include a direct engagement with one's state, a sense of patriotism and national pride, and a desire to promote the state on the international stage and contribute to its national advancement. The pull factors that determine this diplomat's travel activity for diplomacy include the opportunity for international recognition, access to a platform for promoting state interests, and structured dialogue forums that could yield state recognition and positive state branding. Out of McCrae and Costa's (1985) five personality categories, the conscientious personality is the most likely to engage in intentional state-oriented diplomacy, since this form of diplomacy requires consistent engagement with formal procedures, careful planning, and organization.

The Coincidental State-oriented Diplomat

Tourists that engage in state-oriented diplomacy in a coincidental manner are individuals whose primary motivation and reason for travelling is not to conduct diplomacy. Nevertheless, the nature of their travel itinerary and the activities that it entails expose them to opportunities of representing their state, aligning their rhetoric, statements, and activities with the state's interests, and contributing to its positive image among foreign audiences. Examples of this form of coincidental diplomacy through tourism include leisure tourists that can be associated with a specific state – for example by being recognizable public figures or political leaders – and other recreational tourists that engage in political discussions as representatives of their state's position but simply due to their capacity as citizens of that state, without doing so in a formal capacity.

Push factors enabling coincidental state-oriented diplomacy to occur would require a personal interest in political affairs and active engagement with local political affairs at the state level, either through civic engagement or merely from an observer standpoint. An everyday citizen that is up to date with their state's political affairs and holds an interest in discussing this with individuals of foreign states is highly likely to engage in political dialogue and shape the opinions and impressions of foreign audiences about the state they represent through their citizen capacity. The coincidental nature of these exchanges, however, implies that they will occur impromptu, and therefore will not determine the destination selection process in advance.

In the case of coincidental tourist diplomats, pull factors are less relevant since the destination selection is not made on the grounds of conducting diplomacy. Nevertheless, even if the tourist does not have the intention to represent their state's interests, doing so when given the opportunity implies that political factors and the political characteristics of a destination may contribute – even as secondary factors – to destination selection.

Coincidental state-oriented diplomats are likely to illustrate personality traits of extraversion and a tendency to interact with new audiences. As Verma et al. (2017) point out, the extraverted personality category is the one to speak with the most people at a party, indicating the ability of these individuals to easily engage in new social settings, and start conversations with strangers that could lead to coincidental discussions of state affairs and foreign policy.

The Intentional Cosmopolitan Diplomat

Tourist diplomats who intentionally engage with global affairs from a cosmopolitan standpoint are not officially appointed as diplomats by a political agency, unlike the conventional format of state diplomacy. Individual citizens, activists, volunteers, and humanitarian workers could engage in cosmopolitan diplomacy purposefully and consciously as individuals, either by employing professional skills and competencies when doing so, or simply through a personal, interest-based motivation to have a cosmopolitan impact.

This does not mean that intentional cosmopolitan diplomats can only represent themselves as individuals; on the contrary, many non-governmental or supranational organizations whose professional objectives and vision address global causes from a cosmopolitan and transnational angle are likely to engage in international diplomacy with other international entities. Examples of institutional and organizational representation in intentional cosmopolitan diplomacy include transnational collaborations across civil society entities, research centres, universities, charities and foundations, humanitarian agencies, and environmental groups.

Push factors for the intentional cosmopolitan diplomat to engage in short-term travelling would incorporate an interest in global phenomena and global politics, as well as a strong affiliation to cosmopolitan values and worldviews; these characteristics are likely to be complemented by a desire to shape global affairs and contribute to global causes, a strong sense of empathy and membership to a global community, as well as a likely desire to volunteer for causes with a global impact – animal welfare, environmental conservation, human rights, equality, and humanitarian assistance among others. Pull factors of destinations that would allow the intentional cosmopolitan diplomat to engage in contemporary diplomacy would include the ability to actively contribute to a cause, whether by employing diplomacy as a process of negotiating international policy, or by making a political statement through an act or demonstration of international appeal. In this expanded definition of cosmopolitan diplomacy, tourism that enables coordinated action and the exchange of ideas across multiple parties in ways that address cosmopolitan worldviews can also be considered cosmopolitan diplomacy.

Engaging in the unconventional and novel forms of cosmopolitan diplomacy intentionally requires, from a personality perspective, both an elevated level of broadmindedness and an openness to new experiences, as well as aptitude and intellectual engagement to address global affairs as a nonformal, cosmopolitan diplomat. In this regard, the openness personality category is the one closest to performing intentional cosmopolitan diplomacy through tourism.

The Coincidental Cosmopolitan Diplomat

Analogous to the coincidental state-oriented diplomat, the coincidental cosmopolitan diplomat engages in tourist activities for a primary reason other than to conduct diplomacy. Nevertheless, if the tourist embraces cosmopolitan values and is attentive to global affairs, these attributes can play a role when designing a travel experience. Push factors that can shape travel choices may include a desire to engage in global civil society work more actively, to join global movements, or perform cosmopolitan forms of activism and voluntourism, not as incentives to engage in diplomacy, but more so for the purpose of contributing to global welfare. Coincidental cosmopolitan diplomacy can also occur through leisure travel, VFR (visiting friends and relatives), MICE (Meetings, Incentives, Conferences, and Exhibitions), and a variety of specialty travel opportunities, such as honeymoon vacation and gap year travel.

Pull factors for coincidental cosmopolitan diplomacy are not principal in the destination selection of the cosmopolitan tourist since their primary goal is not to engage in diplomacy. Nevertheless, cosmopolitanism as a worldview can be a dominant ideology and one that affects decision-making beyond the purposeful conduct of diplomatic exchanges. To this end, the cosmopolitan tourist diplomat, even when conducting diplomacy coincidentally, could directly be affected by pull factors of destinations that can align with and reinforce cosmopolitan values, while destinations performing political action that challenges or restricts cosmopolitanism could prevent the coincidental cosmopolitan tourist diplomat from choosing them.

The profile of the coincidental cosmopolitan diplomat is characterized by heightened empathy and sensitivity towards global welfare, human rights, and sustainable living, but without the intention to travel for coordinated diplomatic action to address cosmopolitan values and goals. The personality category of McCrae and Costa's (1985) Big Five model that aligns most with the coincidental cosmopolitan diplomat profile is the agreeable one, characterized by flexibility and a lack of personal intention when travelling, but at the same time a desire to engage in community work and voluntourism when given the opportunity.

Discussion

The four categories of tourist-performed diplomacy are re-introduced in Figure 2.2, featuring the personality traits they are distinguished by.

To redefine diplomacy in today's world and acknowledge that diplomacy is substantially more diverse than its traditional state-centric definition, one can argue that tourism today plays a key role in conducting diplomacy. What this chapter presents is that tourism has become a key tool in providing citizens, organizations, states, and other actors with the capacity and the means of conducting diplomacy. To this end, tourism is essential in how diplomacy is conducted today; the less restricted international tourist activity is, the more it enables accessing political actors with which coordinated discussions, negotiations, and political momentum can develop, whether it will serve states or attend to global affairs.

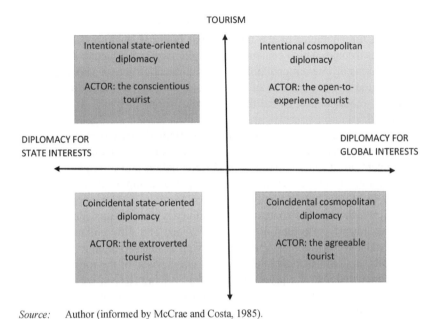

TOURISM

| Intentional state-oriented diplomacy | Intentional cosmopolitan diplomacy |
| ACTOR: the conscientious tourist | ACTOR: the open-to-experience tourist |

DIPLOMACY FOR STATE INTERESTS

DIPLOMACY FOR GLOBAL INTERESTS

| Coincidental state-oriented diplomacy | Coincidental cosmopolitan diplomacy |
| ACTOR: the extroverted tourist | ACTOR: the agreeable tourist |

Source: Author (informed by McCrae and Costa, 1985).

Figure 2.2   Categories of tourist-performed diplomacy

International tourism and the right to travel freely across the globe enables unconventional political actors such as tourists to directly engage with diplomacy. As a result, the international diplomatic stage welcomes new actors and evolves in unprecedented ways. In other words, contemporary tourism shapes contemporary diplomacy by enabling it to further diversify. The key realization is not only that tourism makes diplomacy more diverse, but essentially that it makes diplomacy more inclusive. To this end, tourism becomes a key tool in conducting diplomacy in ways that make the international political stage more accessible and more democratic.

CONCLUSION

This chapter has examined the various ways in which contemporary diplomacy has expanded beyond official state representation and state-performed negotiations. If diplomacy today incorporates discussions by citizens, non-state actors, and civil society more broadly, in a way that can create momentum for political change and new political directions internationally, then one thing that contemporary diplomacy portrays is its ability to incorporate a much wider framework of international discussions across a diversity of political actors.

The growth and expansion of international relations to incorporate a plethora of actors beyond the traditional state-driven scope of the field has vastly expanded the character of the international political stage, and expectedly, the venues through which contemporary diplomacy is conducted. Admittedly, various forms of international political communication across actors are today incorporated into the scheme of contemporary diplomacy, and diplomacy is gradually subdivided to reveal the plethora of forms in which it is currently performed.

The expanding diversity of international diplomatic activity is analogous to the expanding diversity of international tourist activity, which evolved from the conception of mass tourism to its differentiation into multiple categories of niche tourist activity, each reflecting separate components of the tourist market. In the pursuit of identifying which forms of contemporary tourism perform which forms of contemporary diplomacy, this chapter identified and discussed tourist-performed forms of diplomacy and differentiated between intentional and coincidental diplomacy, as well as state-oriented vs. cosmopolitan diplomacy. State-oriented diplomacy is comprised of the forms of diplomacy conducted with the principal goal of advancing state interests, and it is distinguished from diplomatic activity that occurs with a cosmopolitan agenda in mind. The distinction between diplomacy that occurs intentionally and diplomacy that is delivered in a coincidental manner is also a necessary one to record and assess when examining the impact of contemporary diplomacy.

Through the individual level of analysis approach, the chapter identifies four categories of tourist-performed diplomacy and presents how each is shaped by factors of personal motivation and personality traits. The model of tourist-performed diplomacy introduced in this chapter reveals not only the drivers behind it, but more so establishes the role of tourism as a tool for conducting contemporary diplomacy, especially forms of post-state, cosmopolitan diplomacy that involves unconventional diplomacy actors. Through this review of the relationship between tourism and diplomacy, the tourist establishes their ability to expand the scope of contemporary diplomacy and make it more democratic and inclusive.

Additional insights to the relationship between tourism and diplomacy, and the role of the tourist as a non-state actor in transnational resource management are discussed in Chapter 4, "Tourism and peace". Chapter 5 on "Tourism and international security" sets the basis for understanding tourism as a contributor to a variety of international security sectors, which can be positive and conducive in some instances, as well as detrimental in others.

3. Tourism and international security

INTRODUCTION

In a 2007 publication of *Global Issues*, selections by CQ Researcher highlight the key issues of international security the world was facing at the dawn of the new millennium. These included terrorism and armed conflict, democratization, political economy, international law and human rights, and the environment. Interestingly, the latter was discussed in reference not only to climate change, but also to health, making remarks about threatening viruses and the US's pandemic preparedness. Today, as the world recovers from the COVID-19 pandemic, security experts have revisited their priorities: the threat of international terrorist attacks is less imminent, while health and climate change have become primary concerns on a global scale. The CQ Researcher 2022 Edition of *Global Issues* features the topics of global pandemic preparedness in reference to the COVID-19 pandemic, the environment, and the natural gas industry, as well as international development aid.

In an increasingly interconnected world, matters of security have become less nation-specific and more global in scale. The scope of contemporary global security issues expands well beyond military and political threats. The diversity of international security concerns is effectively captured by Buzan et al.'s (1998) framework for security analysis. Buzan et al. argue that international political actors face the likelihood of being exposed to perceived existential threats that can be categorized through five sectors: the military, the environmental, the economic, the societal, and the political. While matters of international security have often been addressed by state actors through foreign policy agendas, addressing security issues of a global nature through isolated actions at the national level could be highly counterproductive. The COVID-19 pandemic is an example of a global security crisis that required coordinated actions from a combination of state and non-state actors. The transnational coordination of policy and action towards global security concerns is, undoubtedly, a vital step in addressing international security in the post-pandemic era.

A discussion of tourism in reference to international security entails both extrinsic factors of security that either confine or enable tourist activity, as well as the ways in which tourist activity affects international security dynamics.

The latter provides a novel approach to the relationship of tourism and international security, as it broadens the scholarly framework of this relationship by examining ways in which tourism stakeholders act as non-state political actors and influence the course of international security. This chapter is therefore set to explore the reciprocal relationship between tourism and international security from diverse perspectives, answering the questions of how international security affects tourism, and how tourism affects international security. In doing so, the section below reviews how tourism has been affected by international security concerns over the past three decades and introduces a selection of theoretical frameworks that explain perceptions of insecurity and global security dynamics.

HOW INTERNATIONAL SECURITY AFFECTS TOURISM: A TIMELINE

International Security in the Post-Cold War Era

The end of the Cold War is a key reference point in the discourse and evolution of international tourism. In 1989, the Berlin Wall dividing East and West Germany was brought down, and symbolically dissolved the Cold War's bipolar political system. Until then, the Cold War divided the world between the Soviet Union and the allies of the communist ideology on the one hand, and the Western liberal ideology led by the United States on the other. The latter proved more resilient and survived as the dominant political ideology shaping international order on a universal scale as the world moved towards the new millennium.

International Relations and International Security scholars were eager to postulate the aftermath of this development and predict the successor of the global scene's bipolar structure. As the end of the Cold War was marked by the dissolution of the Soviet Union, the post-Cold War era granted the United States a status of victory and ideological dominance over the international political system. Krauthammer (1989) signalled the end of the Cold War as an opportunity for transitioning to a unipolar system, which would benefit an increasingly interconnected world – economically and technologically – to achieve security under political unity. Following the dissolution of the Soviet Union, Wohlforth (1999) referred to the United States as the sole surviving superpower and highlighted that a unipolar system is prone to peace and stability. The post-Cold War unipolar international system was characterized by less division and polarization, enabling the United States to spread its neoliberal Western ideology on a universal scale, in the absence of an opposing global power.

A popular text on the world's transition to a post-Cold War Era comes from Francis Fukuyama, who suggested that the end of the Cold War signaled the "end of history" (1989). Fukuyama's reference to history alludes to the dialectics that occurred between the two political ideologies in opposition, forcing them to advance and evolve. The transition of the world into a unipolar world lacks the organic process of evolution that comes from dialectical exchange of information, suggesting that the world had reached a point of political evolution that was sufficient and sustainable.

The reassuring approach taken by Fukuyama is not shared by Huntington and his classic post-Cold War account heralding a "Clash of Civilizations" (1993). The 1993 account projects the eventual transition of international order to a multipolar system, divided into eight civilizations: the Western, the Islamic, the Slavic-Orthodox, the Confucian, the Japanese, the Latin American, Hindu, and the African. Each civilization is characterized by strong bonds of a common identity and culture among their members; characteristics that also differentiate them from one another. According to Huntington, history has indicated that the world's most prolonged and severe conflicts emerge between civilizations. An increasingly interconnected world that will bring heightened interaction and friction between civilizations is, therefore, projected to experience inter-civilizational conflict, a prediction that contradicts the peace and stability that a unipolar world order is expected to bring.

Undoubtedly, the end of the Cold War changed the course of international security and established new realities for international travel. Bianchi and Stephenson (2013) argue that the fall of the Berlin Wall and the end of the Cold War marked a new era of true internationalization of tourist activity, enabling safe access to any destination across the globe. In the spirit of free market politics, capitalism, and Neoliberalism, which were key components of the Western ideology, the post-Cold War period was characterized by uninterrupted access to destinations across the world, an ability that was further enabled by the ever-increasing accessibility and travel choices tourists had.

The internationalization and growth tourism experienced was both due to positive indications towards international security and stability, as well as political will to foster and protect the right to travel internationally in a de-regulated and liberalized manner – reflecting the general principles of liberal international order. According to Bianchi and Stephenson (2013: 16), the United Nations World Tourism Organization (UNWTO) and the World Travel and Tourism Council (WTTC) became strong international advocates of the "inalienable right to travel", further favoring the industry's expansion.

Post-9/11 Era: Non-state Actors and the Emergence of a Multipolar World

Huntington's "Clash of Civilizations" received its most powerful validation in 2001, when the United States, the core of the Western civilization, was attacked by non-state representatives of the Islamic civilization, in what was assessed as an attack on the grounds of identity and political ideology. The 9/11 terrorist attacks in New York were an unprecedented breach of security for the United States, which was at the time considered a global hegemon in international politics. The response to this breach was, expectedly, an imminent increase in security measures across the United States, but also on an international scale, particularly regarding security measures for transnational travel. Security became a central concern in international tourist activity. According to Hall et al. (2004), perceptions of security have a direct influence on tourists' behaviour and their choice of destinations. The perceivably acquired access to any destination that was promoted in the post-Cold War period was abruptly restricted after 9/11, as not all destinations felt sufficiently safe and risk-free.

The 9/11 attack marked a new era for international relations and international security. This new era was characterized not only by increased insecurity, but also by a shift in understanding security threats and perceived risk. Concerns over security extended beyond the state-centric notion of national security, to incorporate the emergence of non-state actors in international politics and to consider security at the individual and global levels (Hall et al., 2004). The War on Terror launched by the United States in response to the 9/11 terrorist attacks highlighted a shift in national security by identifying a non-state enemy and stipulating that international politics no longer occurred on a stage of state actors. Interestingly, two years prior to the 9/11 terrorist attacks, Kaldor (1999) spoke of a shift in international security that is characterized by a transition from old wars that occurred between states to a new type of warfare that includes both state and non-state actors, making it significantly more complex and less predictable. The phenomenon of a new type of warfare was then reaffirmed, both in 2001, and in the subsequent US-led War on Terror.

The post 9/11 period featured a multipolar international system, which included several emerging global powers and a constricted superpower, or as Layne (2006) puts it, a *benign hegemon*. A widely accepted emerging global power of the early twenty-first century was China (Sutter, 2012) to the extent that it was expected to challenge America's hegemony (Feigenbaum, 2008), a prediction that proved accurate in the years that followed. In addition to China, Lennon and Kozlowski (2008) introduce India, Putin's Russia, Japan, and the European Union as the global powers shaping international security in the new millennium.

From an analogous perspective of a multipolar world, Buzan and Wæver (2003) introduce a geopolitical approach to international security through the Regional Security Complex Theory (RSCT). Buzan and Wæver identify the Regional Security Complexes of North America, South America, Europe, Central Africa, Southern Africa, Middle East, Post-Soviet, South Asia, and East Asia, while they also identify the Asian supercomplex. Each complex's dynamics are defined by whether it includes regional powers – standard complex – or a global power/superpower (centered security complex/supercomplex). The Regional Security Complex framework additionally incorporates the buffer and insulator countries; the former refers to a state or mini complex *within* a security complex, creating a buffer for power dynamics within that complex, while the latter regulates security dynamics *between* security complexes. Turkey and Afghanistan are contemporary examples of insulator countries, standing between regional security complexes, but without being incorporated into any of them. The RSCT approach stands opposite Huntington's "Clash of Civilizations", as Huntington's approach defines international security at the borderlines between civilizations, whereas RSCT argues that international security dynamics are set within each regional complex and not between them. Despite their contrasting approaches, both accounts admit a multipolar balance of power that sets the basis of international security.

The post-9/11 era posed significant security threats to international tourist activity. The threat of unpredictable terrorist attacks hindered the perceived safety of travel destinations and was of particular concern to tourist audiences. According to Araña and León (2008), who examined the aftermath of the 9/11 terrorist attacks, tourist preferences are directly affected by a terrorist attack and experience a *terror shock* that significantly lowers a destination's tourism traffic in the months following an attack. Their study also revealed that terrorist activity had a more lasting negative impact in destinations with a predominantly-Islamic population, such as Tunisia and Turkey, in comparison to non-Islamic destinations.

Due to a combination of both political and military security concerns, the likelihood of a terrorist attack proved to directly affect the tourism and hospitality sectors and made tourist zones and hospitality infrastructure significantly fragile to the threat of an imminent terrorist attack. As Henderson et al. (2010) reaffirm, hotels are attractive targets for terrorist attacks, with luxury hotels demonstrating increased vulnerability. Wernick and Von Glinow (2012) add that Western-branded luxury hotels had been a preferred target of post-9/11 terrorist attacks, specifically over the examined period of 2002–2009. During this period, the frequency of terrorist attacks had more than doubled, from 30 to 62, and attacks to Western-branded luxury hotels accounted for ten out of the 62 attacks recorded globally.

The subjectivity of perceived risk in international security is fundamental in understanding the disparity between absolute and perceived risk, with perceived risk being the individual's assessed level of uncertainty and threat in any given situation. The subjective assessment of risk is what eventually determines tourist decision-making, yet this subjectivity creates a deviation from the actual risk present. This realization is directly relevant to the Copenhagen's School concept of securitization, which explains the process through which an existential threat is subjectively constructed.

The securitization perspective, or the concept of securitization, is provided by the Copenhagen School of Security Studies, offering a constructivist rather than a materialist approach to the study of international security. It refers to the process in which one event or phenomenon is prioritized over others and formally presented as an existential threat to a referent object, X. An existential threat can be formally declared, often via a public statement or speech that is performed by a securitizing actor. For the threat declaration to be successful, the securitizing actor must be a reliable and influential political figure, often the leader of a state. The referent object to be facing the existential threat must directly affiliate with the securitizing actor and it can be as narrow as a state's economic performance, or as wide as the survival of humanity.

The securitization perspective questions the objectivity of threats to the security of political agents, as their saliency is determined and manipulated by the actors acknowledging the threat (Buzan et al., 1998). Defining an issue as an existential threat to a referent object in question enables the securitizing actor to take advantage of the threat's political effects and act in means that would otherwise be considered unsuitable (ibid.). In other words, the securitization perspective suggests the importance of considering a threat as a political construction, and hence acknowledging the possibility of its subsequent political manipulation. With the threat of international terrorism being associated with Islamic terrorist groups, the perceived risk of non-Muslim tourists visiting Islamic destinations significantly increased in the 9/11 aftermath, indicating the securitization of the Islamic world as a potential threat to non-Islamic audiences, or what was often expressed as Islamophobia.

A destination is prone to being securitized based on its dominant identities making the perceived destination image as less safe or safer accordingly. A destination's perceived safety can also be affected by the tourist audience in question; audiences of a welcomed identity may feel safer to visit Destination X, whereas an audience that has been negatively targeted by Destination X may perceive it as less safe and will be less likely to visit it. The ability of tourists to feel safe in their visited destinations is not only a matter that was affecting Islamic audiences during the post-9/11 era. Demographic segmentations of the tourist market may refer to – among other identities – religion, ethnicity, gender, age, and sexuality. LGBT tourist audiences, for example, have been identified as one of the most vulnerable and discriminated-against audiences in the industry (Usai et al., 2022). Interestingly, a tourist destination that is perceived to be LGBT-inclusive is considered safer by potential visitors, regardless of their affiliation with the LGBT community (Ram et al., 2019). Ram et al.'s study was conducted with the case study of Tel Aviv and indicated that, as an LGBT-inclusive destination, Tel Aviv was considered safe by visitors despite a recent terrorist attack, suggesting that destination inclusivity can positively affect security perceptions even in geopolitically unstable or terrorist-prone destinations.

According to Yang and Nair (2014) perceived risk in tourist activity is a key factor in determining travel decision-making and destination choices. Nevertheless, while for many tourists, ensuring safety and security is catalytic in travel intention, for others a level of risk can be perceived as desirable. Korstanje and Clayton (2012) point out that security and risk do not affect tourist choices in a linear way, but in a subjective one. Politicized and securitized threats such as international terrorism affect tourist travel choices more severely than forms of organized crime and domestic terrorism, even if the latter occurs on a larger scale (ibid.). One can argue that the risk of prosecution due to factors of gender and sexuality is a politicized, and in certain cases a securitized threat, that directly informs tourist decision-making for affected audiences.

Post-pandemic Era: the Increasing Fragility of International Security

The United States' hegemonic decline and the emergence of a multipolar world were heralded throughout the two decades that followed the 9/11 attacks. This presumption was further reinforced during Donald Trump's presidency of the United States. During this time, the US refurbished its foreign policy and prioritized national security over global influence and international order and stability. According to Cooley and Nexon (2020), the Trump Presidency adopted a zero-sum approach to security that diminished the value of international alliances and confined the ability of the United States to foster international security through the establishment of a liberal international order. The lack of a post-Cold War "Pax Romana" under the hegemony of the United States in a peace-prone, unipolar international structure became even more evident at the dawn of the 2020 pandemic crisis, which lacked coordinated action and a universal response for preventing the spread of the COVID-19 virus (ibid.). In the international tourism industry, the pandemic revealed two matters of priority to be addressed in the post-pandemic era: resilience and equity.

The pandemic had a direct and unfathomable impact on the tourism industry internationally, both by posing a major and unpredicted crisis, as well as by establishing prolonged uncertainty over its duration, discourse, and aftermath. It was, therefore, crucial to evaluate the resilience of the sector and its people by assessing their ability to recover and resume the sector's operations. Gössling et al. (2021) emphasize that the sector exposed the increased vulnerability of lower-paid jobs in tourism, as well as lower-income destinations. In both cases, evidence and projections indicated that these two categories were affected negatively in a disproportionate manner. Establishing community resilience on a global scale and bridging the resilience gap across professionals in tourism is crucial in making the international tourism industry more resistant to future crises and, as such, more sustainable. A key priority for achieving resilience is, therefore, to achieve equity within the sector, and across destinations.

Benjamin et al. (2020) highlight that the pandemic interrupted the heavily unsustainable business-as-usual model of the international tourism industry. The severe travel restrictions and social distancing regulations resulted in the loss of an estimated 50 million tourism-related jobs globally (ibid.). While many referred to the post-pandemic end goal as our ability to collectively return to normal, it is doubtful whether the "normal" status of the tourism industry is desirable, or even applicable. Benjamin et al. (2020) argue that the capitalist and consumerist nature of tourism had enabled it to grow into an unsustainable international practice that lacked an ethical framework, making it a non-viable normal to return to.

International tourism has been flagged as a key contributor to the spread of COVID-19 and a catalyst in turning it into a pandemic with severe health, social, and economic consequences globally (Benjamin et al., 2020). More specifically, in addition to mass travel patterns that amplified the pandemic's global spread within a matter of weeks, governmental authorities underestimated the pandemic's severity and refused to restrict accessibility to certain destinations (ibid.). At the same time, holidaymakers appeared unwilling to compromise leisure and abide by pandemic-related regulations such as the use of face masks and social distancing.

The pandemic has highlighted the reciprocal nature of the relationship between tourism and international security. While health security concerns severely affected international tourism operations throughout the pandemic's duration and beyond, tourism itself was a catalyst in the spread, duration, and consequences of the virus. To this end, any discussion concerning the relationship between tourism and international security should both explore the ways in which matters of international security affect international tourist activity and, most importantly, examine the overlooked ways in which patterns of tourist activity affect international security dynamics.

HOW TOURISM AFFECTS INTERNATIONAL SECURITY

Tourism is undoubtedly affected by international security, and more specifically the level of perceived security that pertains to specific destinations. Through the review of international security concerns in previous eras, it is evident that the "inalienable right to travel" (Bianchi and Stephenson, 2013: 16) has been challenged by both tangible and intangible security threats, resulting in some destinations being less accessible than others, and some groups of travellers feeling less safe than others.

An emerging structural analysis in International Relations and one that directly informs international security is that of networks. The network approach aims to shed light on the interconnectedness and often interdependency of international political actors, and as such to understand the relations and dynamics between them more comprehensively. According to Hoff and Ward (2004), a key contribution of network analysis is to avoid the assumption that the decision-making and activity of international political actors are isolated phenomena, independent of other actions on the international stage. At the same time, Hafner-Burton et al. (2009) warn that if network analysis is not conducted comprehensively, inconclusive and inaccurate assertions may arise.

The internationalization of security issues has brought international security to the forefront of national agendas. At the same time, international security has been exposed to a growing diversification of security themes, growing beyond tangible state enemies, and often fighting intangible or invisible enemies – such as pandemics and environmental destruction. This observation makes Buzan et al.'s (1998) security framework increasingly relevant and applicable in the post-pandemic era, when existential security threats emerge from across the framework's sectors. This framework is, therefore, utilized as a key reference for analyzing the ways in which tourism affects international security. The analysis below employs the five principal areas of international security – namely the military, political, societal, economic, and environmental – to establish a comprehensive understanding of the tourism-security relationship.

Military Security

Historically, state actors, military alliances such as NATO, and international organizations such as the UN have used military intervention in territories that are considered rogue with the aim of restoring international security and stability. Military interventions have been seen both as an effort to protect civilians in danger, as well as an opportunity for the intervening power to gain political control over the other state's territory and resources. The latter has frequently been criticized as an unethical motive behind military interventions, specifically when delivered unilaterally by one state actor against another.

A less controversial form of intervention is the UN's peacekeeping operations, which focus on creating ceasefire zones and halting violence, rather than engaging in the use of direct military force. UN peacekeeping operations include the employment of military, police, and civilian peacekeepers, and abide by three principles: (1) consent of the parties, (2) impartiality, and (3) use of force only for self-defence or to defend the UN mandate (United Nations, 2022a). Rourke and Boyer (2008) speak of the limited effectiveness the UN peacekeeping forces carry due to these three principles and the restricted span of authority they have. An additional concern they raise is that UN peacekeeping missions and the number of troops employed are often confined by state interests that shape decisions taken at the Security Council level.

While foreign military intervention raised political and philosophical concerns over the right to infringe a nation's sovereignty, human rights violations introduced the question of whether the international community's commitment to protecting state sovereignty is greater than its responsibility to protect citizens when their governmental representatives fail to do so. The Responsibility to Protect, or R2P, was first introduced at the 2005 UN World Summit as a global effort to end mass atrocities (Bellamy, 2009). The anarchic status of the international stage enabled phenomena of human right violations within state borders, leaving the international community to choose between protecting human rights through intervention or upholding the state's right to sovereignty. The Responsibility to Protect principle advocated for the right to violate state sovereignty at times when the sovereign state is unable to protect its citizens from imminent threat.

The restoration of security in the military sector is, overwhelmingly, a conventional form of state-centric political discourse. It involves state actors and institutions with a state membership and leaves little room for non-state actors to engage in any form of military activity for defending and restoring security – other than paramilitary groups and terrorists – on a domestic or transnational level. It is, therefore, not surprising that international tourist activity does not engage with conventional forms of security in the military sector and has been historically left out of scholarly conversations on international security.

Despite this, tourism stakeholders have been at the forefront of the currently ongoing war in Ukraine, which commenced after Russia's military intervention in February 2022. More specifically, the Peer-to-Peer (P2P) accommodation platform, Airbnb, launched its support to the people fleeing Ukraine within four days of the war's launch on 24 February through three immediate actions: (1) it blocked Russia and its ally Belarus from the platform entirely, (2) it enabled direct fundraising for Ukraine-based platform users, by encouraging other users to book rentals in Ukraine for monetary humanitarian assistance and not for staying, and (3) it launched a campaign to host Ukrainian refugees in Airbnb rentals internationally – with the voluntary consent of international hosts (Airbnb, 2022). The platform also pledged to financially support the housing initiative and match the support of its members by adding number of stays, while also waiving any Airbnb fees (ibid.).

The P2P platform received an overwhelming global response from its users. In a matter of days, and after online influencers supported Airbnb's idea to send direct funding through rental booking in Ukraine, the total booking value – and direct assistance offered – reached $2 million (Akhtar, 2022). With regards to the refugee housing initiative, Politico reports that by mid-March, approximately two weeks after the initiative was announced, more than 36,000 Airbnb hosts had signed up to provide housing to Ukrainians fleeing the war (Haeck, 2022). Airbnb CEO, Brian Chesky, also reached out to the states of Germany, Poland, Romania, Hungary, the UN's migration agency, and Jewish aid association HIAS to ensure optimal stakeholder coordination (ibid.).

Airbnb's involvement with the war in Ukraine is not the platform's first engagement with humanitarian assistance to refugees. The company has set up a Refugee Fund, which has already assisted 20,000 Afghan refugees in finding a temporary home (Airbnb, 2022). The Airbnb refugee initiative is introduced on its website under the headline "In times of crisis, be a host" (ibid.).

The platform's unprecedented and immediate engagement with Ukraine's invasion and refugee crisis illuminated the role of tourism stakeholders in scenarios of warfare and military crisis and suggested tourism's political capacity as a non-state actor in war. The Airbnb initiative did not escape from media analysis and criticism. Vox highlighted that fundraising through Airbnb means reaching Ukrainians through selected elites – the platform's hosts – and it does not guarantee any humanitarian assistance to members of the population that have no access to the platform or the Internet (Akhtar, 2022) – a share of the population that is even more vulnerable in times of crisis. Politico, in review of the refugee housing initiative, raised the concerns that short-term stays do not guarantee housing for refugees in the long term, while a speedy refugee–host matching process that lacks any background checks may endanger either hosts or refugees (Haeck, 2022). This criticism, however, does not dispute the magnitude of Airbnb's influence in addressing the refugee crisis imminently and collectively, an initiative that was soon followed by other local P2P platforms for refugee hosting, such as Takecarebnb (ibid.).

Political Security

Airbnb's direct involvement in the Russia–Ukraine war is not only a response to military security, but to political security as well. In 1998, Buzan et al.

defined political security as the "organizational stability of social order" (1998: 141). Through this definition of political security, it can be argued that Airbnb provided new structures for humanitarian assistance and crisis management on an individual, state, and regional level, directly contributing to the organizational stability of social order at a time of crisis and transition. It comes as no surprise that tourism infrastructure, offering channels of transnational mobility globally, could be utilized to support nonvoluntary transnational movement – such as displacement from conflict – and enhance political stability.

Airbnb's success for international political mobilization reverts to Kaldor's notion of global civil society. As Kaldor (2003) explains, local civil society movements developed a global capacity primarily due to two factors: (1) the creation of connections between like-minded movements across countries, and (2) the emergence of the international human rights framework and legislation, providing a common reference point for human rights activism. In the case of Airbnb and its three-fold response to the Russia–Ukraine war, the platform was utilized as a channel for political activism in support of the invaded Ukrainian population, engaging individual users of the Airbnb platform from across the globe, who were engaging in a conscious act of political activism.

Looking beyond political activism, short-term travel can also generate political and social impact in the visited destination when it involves the visitors' sociopolitical engagement in a professional capacity. An example that illustrates this form of tourist input is *peacebuilding tourism*, or "the professionally motivated peace tourists that engage in peace-oriented travel specifically due to their professional capacity" (Antoniou, 2022). Professionals that directly engage with the sociopolitical dynamics of a destination through short-term travel offer a more targeted input that can be distinguished from the engagement offered by active citizens and transnational activism. In the example of peacebuilding tourism, peacebuilding professionals engage with the conflict resolution initiatives and post-conflict transition of a destination, offer input and best practices for effective reconciliation, and have the capacity to provide locals with the tools necessary to engage in grassroots reconciliation, as well as conflict management and settlement on a leadership level. To this end, and in addition to the growing influence of global civil society movements, selected forms of niche tourism can have a direct impact on a destination's political stability, and as such its political security, especially in periods of conflict and post-conflict transition.

Societal Security

Societal security refers to social or collective identities and the extent to which they are considered under threat. Severely securitized identities experience perceived threats that put in question the very existence of that identity and not simply its organizational capacity – as is the case with political security. Societal security concerns can therefore escalate to incorporate restrictions on freedom of expression with regards to an individual's identity, such as religion, gender, race, ethnicity, or ideology.

Examples of societal insecurity in travel come from destinations that are deemed unsafe for certain social identities to be expressed. Countries that penalize homosexuality would be an unsafe destination for members of the LGBT community, and in an analogous manner, communities with ongoing identity-based conflict – religious, racial, or ethnic – could expose travellers of certain identities to a higher risk of violence or confrontation. The hospitality industry has made significant steps towards attending to the increased vulnerability of LGBT travellers, through the promotion of LGBT tourism as a niche tourist activity, and the delivery of LGBT travel fairs and events to promote safe and inclusive destinations. Numerous international hospitality brands have issued inclusive branding and statements of support to diversity, establishing higher levels of societal security in the destinations represented. The branding of LGBT-friendly destinations has also been influenced by pro-LGBT messages and events, such as annual pride parades and celebrations.

Snellings (2019) discusses Tel Aviv's brand as an LGBT-friendly destination, often referred to as a gay capital globally that indicates a safe and fun destination for members of sexual minority groups. This brand has established a notable LGBT tourism industry in Tel Aviv that offers significant economic revenue to the city. In addition to the economic benefits, Tel Aviv's gay-friendly destination brand has also provided a haven of acceptance and freedom of expression for local sexual minorities, having a direct impact on local societal security. Nevertheless, while the impact of the industry on LGBT societal security has been significant for Tel Aviv, the rest of the country continues to be exposed to restrictions of LGBT rights, establishing Tel Aviv as a bubble of LGBT acceptance not echoed elsewhere in Israel (ibid.).

Societal security has also, to a great extent, been endorsed by the establishment of travel networks such as Couchsurfing and Servas International. According to Antoniou (2022) the Couchsurfing hosts network in ethnically partitioned Cyprus brought local hosts from across the divide together and provided a common space of dialogue and resilience on an island experiencing a politically intractable and divisive ethnic conflict.

Travel networks often acknowledge their commitment to intercultural respect and peaceful coexistence. The Couchsurfing network states on its website: "We envision a world made better by travel and travel made richer by connection. Couchsurfers share their lives with the people they encounter, fostering cultural exchange and mutual respect" (Couchsurfing, 2022). Servas International states that "the purpose of the network is to help build world peace, goodwill and understanding by providing opportunities for personal contacts among people of different cultures, backgrounds and nationalities" (Servas International, 2022).

The shared identity of being a Couchsurfer, Servas member or a member of a network of fellow travellers provides a framework of safe interaction irrespective of ethnic, racial, or religious backgrounds. The travel network identity that clarifies respect towards diverse ethnic, religious, or other politically contested identities provides a safe space for interaction across destinations, contributing to the hosts and visitors' level of perceived social security, as well as enabling their safe and positive interactions with members of other identity groups that could otherwise be addressed with skepticism or prejudice. As mentioned in Chapter 2, positive and meaningful intercultural encounters through tourism have the capacity to increase cultural literacy, and thus increase perceived societal security.

Economic Security

A lack of economic security directly affects international tourist activity. This was evident during the financial crisis that unfolded after 2008, as well as during the 2020 COVID-19 pandemic. At the same time, however, it is possible for international tourist activity to shape international economics, and in turn ease concerns of economic security, whether on a national or on a regional level.

Examples discussed within the military, political, and societal sectors of security illustrated tourism's positive impact on the enhancement of inter-national security. Despite this, certain forms of tourist-led economic activity have been flagged as detrimental to resilience and raise sector-specific security concerns. The contribution of tourism to economic development and, as such, to increased economic stability globally has been extensively discussed in Chapter 1 on international development. What has not been as thoroughly examined, however, are two areas of economic security concern: (1) the impact of vacation rentals on property rates and rent, and (2) the dependency of destinations on tourism as a primary source of GDP.

Short-term vacation rentals, which have become increasingly popular and available, have been directly linked to high rent inflation in popular tourist des-tinations such as Barcelona (Mendoza and Russo, 2022). While vacation rental platforms like Airbnb have provided a fresh and affordable accommodation option to travellers internationally, the vacation rentals trend has increased the cost of living for locals while diminishing their ability to access basic services (ibid.). This phenomenon has led locals to leave homes that are no longer affordable, causing gentrification and social exclusion.

Rental-related inflation can be detrimental to the perceived economic security of host populations as they could drive not only rental prices, but also service and product prices upwards, affecting local purchasing power. Even when locals receive direct income from the tourist industry, economic security can be put at risk, especially in cases of a destination's high dependency on tourism-generated revenue. As Sharpley and Ussi (2014) clarify, countries that are popular tourist destinations are also the ones most susceptible to economic dependency on the tourism industry. In cases of high economic dependency on tourism, which is often observed in small island developing states (SIDS), unequal socio-economic and spatial development is highly likely (ibid.). According to Sharpley (2012), there are states within the SIDS category that show records of poor governance and an inability to utilize tourism revenue for improving social welfare and local industry capacities. Developing states with poor governance records that receive significant revenue from tourism are therefore not necessarily absorbing foreign capital for their gradual development, but instead perpetuating a dynamic of inequality, dependency, and high economic insecurity.

Environmental Security

The climate crisis has brought the security of the environment to the forefront of international security concerns, as a decaying ecosystem poses an imminent threat to human existence. The solution that has been coined after decades of ecosystem examination and attempts for global environmental conservation is to achieve environmental sustainability, or in other words to establish a level of human activity that does not exceed the earth's resource capacities and allows future generations to access the environment in a similar or improved state. Achieving intergenerational equity does not only apply to ecosystem conservation, but also serves a broader framework for sustainable development. The latter refers to the ability of humans to balance economic development, environmental conservation, and societal welfare in a way that achieves economic, societal, and environmental security through sustainability, and thus eliminates existential threats in all three sectors.

Sustainable development has been criticized for being a far too ambiguous concept to measure, evaluate, and achieve. Sharpley (2020) highlights that economic development contradicts environmental conservation and it is utopic to expect the two to occur simultaneously. Contemporary international tourist activity has outstandingly confirmed this criticism: tourism is a key international industry for global economic development, and at the same time a direct threat to global environmental security.

According to Lenzen et al. (2018), in 2013, the trillion-dollar global tourism industry was responsible for 8% of the global greenhouse gas emissions, making tourism a carbon-intensive practice. Tourism transportation emissions through aviation and shipping continue to increase and are not subjected to the international standards of carbon emission reductions set by the 2015 Paris Agreement on climate change (ibid.). In a 2014 study, Sun calculated that international aviation accounted for 28% of tourism's total carbon footprint, a figure that is especially important for island destinations that rely heavily – if not entirely – on aviation for tourist accessibility.

In addition to tourism transportation being a major carbon emissions contributor, a form of tourist activity known as *last-chance tourism* has been gaining popularity and is posing a direct threat to fragile ecosystems and animal species threatened with extinction. Last-chance tourism, as the name reveals, is tourist activity motivated by the belief that a present travel opportunity to see a species, landscape, or natural phenomenon in person may not exist in the future because of climate change and environmental destruction. Kucukergin and Gürlek (2020) examine the motivation of seeing a place or attraction before it disappears and identify that the notion of a last-chance experience positively contributes to a tourist's place satisfaction.

A prominent example of last-chance tourism is travel with the purpose of seeing polar bears in their natural environment (Lemelin et al., 2010). A symbol of the fight against climate change, the prospect of seeing polar bears in person before going extinct has intrigued last-chance tourists, who are willing to travel far and pay thousands in Canadian dollars to achieve this (ibid.). Ironically, the carbon-intensive nature of this activity directly contributes to the degradation of the polar bear habitats and increases the likelihood of polar bear extinction, a factor that does not appear to affect last-chance tourist motivation (ibid.).

Tourist decision-making and consumption choices are a primary determinant of tourism's carbon footprint. Nevertheless, the percentage of tourists that planned their travel in consideration of their carbon footprint was recorded to be as low as 1% (Skidmore, 2008). To the contrary, the same study indicated that cost was a more important determinant in travel plans, at a share of 43%. Tourism consumption can be affected by a range of factors, including the availability of eco-friendly alternatives at comparable prices. In the absence of eco-friendly options, tourists – including environmentally-aware individuals – face a higher possibility of engaging in non-sustainable consumption, using carbon-emitting transportation and accommodation, and relying on single-use packaged food and beverage options. One can argue that the temporary nature of tourist experiences makes it easier for tourists to temporarily deviate from environmentally friendly and sustainable practices they have established in their place of residence, where options and investments on long-term sustainable practice may be numerous in comparison. According to Hall (2014), absolute emissions from tourism are only expected to increase, unless a radical shift towards green alternatives is achieved to enable tourism's green growth.

Marzouki et al. (2012) utilize ecological footprint analysis as a method of measuring the environmental impact of various forms of tourism. They define ecological footprint as a way "to measure how the human appropriation of the earth's resources relates to the carrying capacity of the earth" (2012: 123) and apply this to tourist activity to detect at which levels tourism can be environmentally sustainable. Surprisingly, their application of ecological footprint analysis to compare ecotourism to mass tourism reveals that destinations of ecotourism, a responsible tourist practice to areas of environmental conservation (Ruhanen and Axelsen, 2022), have a larger footprint than mass tourism destinations. This observation is heavily derived from the fact that ecotourism involves long-distance travel, especially to southern countries, making it only a partially sustainable practice. At the same time, however, Marzouki et al. (2012) highlight that mass tourism is responsible for irreversible environmental deterioration, whereas this is not the case with ecotourism.

Health Security?

Health security has not been identified as a separate sector in Buzan et al.'s (1998) framework of security analysis, and scholarship has viewed health as a component of environmental security. Extant research has thus far verified a direct correlation between environmental quality and human health, suggesting that health security cannot be achieved in the absence of environmental security and sustainability. Mishra et al. (2021) warn that anthropogenic activities have disrupted the balanced coexistence of humans, animals, and the environment, leading to unprecedented outbreaks of zoonotic diseases, such as the COVID-19 pandemic. In a post-pandemic world, health security is expected to be a priority, and addressed through environmental sustainability. Immediate steps to be taken include responses to "habitat fragmentation, deforestation, biodiversity loss, intensive agriculture and livestock farming, uncontrolled urbanization, and pollution" (ibid.). Ironically, health insecurity caused by the COVID-19 outbreak was detrimental to the international tourism industry, yet the carbon-intensive nature of tourism makes it a lead cause of environmentally unsustainable practices that led to the outbreak in the first place.

ACHIEVING INTERNATIONAL SECURITY THROUGH TOURISM

There are two ways in which tourism is set to be a key contributor to international security: the first is by enhancing security on a local, transnational, and global scale, and the second is by posing direct threat to security across sectors. As observed through the sector-based security analysis of international tourism conducted within this chapter, the military, political, and societal sectors of security have benefited from certain forms of tourist activity, whereas other aspects of tourism raise instability and security concerns for the economic and environmental sectors. Differentiating between positive and negative impacts of tourism on international security enables tourism stakeholders to endorse the positive and restrict the negative, establishing a framework of international tourism conduct that enhances international security.

Environmental Security: Increasing Environmental Consciousness and Measuring Ecological Footprint

Tourist environmental consciousness is a key factor in determining whether any tourist activity will be detrimental to the environment or not. Kucukergin and Gürlek argue that even in last chance tourism, which is linked to environmental deterioration for the most fragile ecosystems, environmentally conscious tourists have the capacity to confine the ecological footprint of their tourist activity with responsible waste management and informed engagement with the destination. At the same time, they can increase awareness for themselves and others about the state of urgency of fragile destinations (ibid.). Media and social media outlets can contribute to environmental consciousness and influence tourist decision-making by sharing examples of irresponsible behavior at last chance tourism destinations and highlighting the need to avoid such actions.

Marzouki et al. (2012) introduce Ecological Footprint Analysis as a tool that can measure whether a tourist activity can cause environmental deterioration, and to what extent. More specifically, the EFA tool measures "the area required to support a certain lifestyle" and compares it to the area available provided by the destination (ibid.). This method calculates "the appropriation of biologically productive areas by individuals or nations" and can indicate whether any given tourist consumption activity and lifestyle is environmentally sustainable.

In addition to the EFA tool, Mancini et al. (2018) established a customized Ecological Footprint methodology accounting for the main four tourism services: Accommodation, Food and Drinks, Activity and Service, and Mobility and Transfer. Analogous to EFA, Mancini et al.'s EF (Ecological Footprint) methodology provides a calculation of the ecological footprint generated through tourism demand, comparing it to the biocapacity (BC) provided by the supply side of the destination. The ability of the destination's nature to regenerate after biologically productive areas have been engaged for human consumption – specifically tourist consumption – would make the supply and demand exchange sustainable. Gössling et al. (2012) go a step further to introduce water footprint recommendations to specifically address freshwater usage in tourism infrastructure and proactively solidify water security in tourism destinations with water scarcity. The 2012 article calculates water footprint for both direct and indirect water usage (including water requirements in food production, infrastructural development, and energy use) to comprehensively account for the quantities of water allocated to serve tourists – whose numbers often exceed local population levels.

Measuring the ecological and water footprint of each type of tourist activity enables sustainable tourism to become a tangible, measurable, and achievable goal; one that local and transnational policymakers can reach through policies that restrict the carbon-intensive nature of tourism and provide realistic alternatives. According to Sharpley (2021) the key to sustainable tourism production and consumption lies in its effective regulation, which sets boundaries for tourist activity that do not exceed the ecosystem's resource capacity. Nevertheless, regulation alone cannot guarantee a sustainable and thriving international industry if it does not provide clean energy alternatives that can aid the transition of international tourist activity to a carbon neutral industry.

Economic Security: Achieving Sustainable Development

The epitome of sustainable development is the balanced co-delivery of economic progress, environmental conservation, and social welfare. Achieving economic development without accounting for resource constraints, consequences on health, and forms of social inequality has proven to only work on a temporary basis. To achieve economic security is, therefore, determined by the ability to establish enduring economic systems whose practices do not contradict environmental or social sustainability. The example of Airbnb rentals and their economic impact on saturated urban tourist destinations such as Barcelona is an example of the industry's unsustainable development in a manner that did not account for social sustainability and welfare. Addressing the latter will inform the industry and its various hospitality stakeholders on how to establish healthy structures of accommodation provision, regulated by their ability to achieve low ecological footprints.

Sustainable development provides a reliable framework for economic security on both a local and a global scale. It has been criticized for being an ambiguous and unrealistic concept (Sharpley, 2020), and indeed, it does not fully provide instructions as to *how* it can be achieved; the answer can be very different for each economic system. Nevertheless, when employing the principle of simultaneous progress for the ecological, economic, and social pillars, it is evident that those actors deviating from the model of sustainable development the most – such as SIDS dependent on tourist income – are at greater risk of economic insecurity. The matter of *how* a SID state can achieve sustainable development – whether this will be a matter of local governance, global input, or civil society action – needs to be discussed further beyond the premises of this chapter.

CONCLUSION

International security had been traditionally defined by military interventions and coercive action across state actors on the global stage. In the past few decades, the military monopoly of international security concerns has been breached, with the field vastly evolving beyond the military framework. This chapter utilized Buzan et al.'s (1998) security framework for analysis that identifies five sectors of international security that can each be threatened on an existential level and can be addressed through political acts.

Political acts that affect international security within the military, political, societal, economic, and environmental sectors have been exponentially undertaken by tourism actors and stakeholders. Evaluating the impact of tourism on security through the traditional, military-oriented framework points to the emergence of non-traditional tourism actors, and particularly international accommodation platforms such as Airbnb. The ability of Airbnb to engage in the Russia–Ukraine war of 2022, and within a matter of four days establish routes of humanitarian assistance, fundraising, and refugee shelter for Ukrainians fleeing Russia's military invasion, puts Airbnb – and traveller platforms altogether – in the spotlight for non-state actor intervention in warfare.

This ad-hoc response to military insecurity complements the long-term phenomenon of global civil society movements which, through tourist activity, can raise awareness and mobilize for securing political order and fostering community resilience. This has again been achieved through the structures of travel networks with a recognizable in-group identity, such as Couchsurfing. While network analysis has thus far been used to inform state partnerships and transnational alliances for international security, it should expand to incorporate travel networks and platforms, whose political and humanitarian input has elevated them as key stakeholders in military and political security.

In addition to the political and military sectors, tourism is seen to affect societal security and create momentum that enhances social inclusivity and equality. These factors are central to societal sustainability and, as a result, to sustainable development. Nevertheless, tourism has also been flagged as a direct contributor to international insecurity, specifically regarding the economic and environmental sectors. The international industry's exponential growth followed the free-market model and prioritized the right of every individual to travel, resulting in unplanned infrastructural development, grave use of environmental resources, and unsustainable structures of economic dependency. Luckily, tourism practice is today more informed and conscious than its past discourse and has the opportunity – through its state and non-state stakeholders – to consider its economic and environmental impact more responsibly.

4. Tourism and peace

INTRODUCTION

The previous chapters of this book embarked on an exploration of tourism as a political act, and more specifically as a form of international relations. This reconceptualization of international tourist activity from the perspective of international relations deconstructed the conventional approaches to the study of Tourism and identified the ways in which international tourist activity bares socio-political consequences, whether these are intentional or at times coincidental. In Chapter 1, examining the relationship between tourism and international development revealed that cosmopolitan ideologies and indicators of cultural literacy can make an informative distinction between the forms of tourism that contribute to sustainable development – as outlined through the Sustainable Development Goals agenda – and tourist activity that contradicts it. Chapter 2 introduced the concept of cosmopolitan diplomacy as an emerging type of diplomatic discourse that is inclusive and involves unconventional political actors, such as tourists and tourism stakeholders. Chapter 3 established a relationship between tourism and international security, and discussed how international security has affected tourism, as well as how tourism informs five distinct sectors of international security.

This chapter follows the book's pattern of examining tourism's relationship with a specific international political process or end goal and considers the relationship and contribution of tourism to peace. Peace, like development, diplomacy, and security, has the capacity to be conceptualized both as a process and as an end goal, but it can be challenged by the blurry lines around its definition, making it subjective and less straightforward to the audiences wishing to pursue it. Scholarly discussions around peace have conventionally placed it within the realm of conflict resolution, introducing it as the outcome of conflict management and peacebuilding processes. Admittedly, to build peace first requires acknowledging its absence, which occurs most often in the presence of conflict. Nevertheless, to comprehensively examine and understand peace, it is imperative to see it as a stand-alone phenomenon and not as the product of a specific practice – conflict resolution. It is possible to detect peace in communities that have not necessarily engaged in its intentional formation through recovery, reconciliation, and transition from conflict. This realization enables scholars to look beyond conflict resolution and examine the dynamics of peace through multiple and diverse avenues. This chapter does so by exploring how peace can be achieved, fostered, sustained, and protected by employing an amalgamation of perspectives and primarily diplomacy, development, and security. In doing so, the chapter delves further into the relationship between tourism and peace, to assess the contribution of tourism to peace both within but more so beyond the scope of conflict resolution.

Peace has conventionally been defined as the end goal of peacebuilding and reconciliation processes; the desired outcome sought in conditions of conflict (Farmaki, 2017). When peace is not achieved, it is assumed that conflict endures, and that conflict obtains a protracted or intractable status. The interconnected relationship between conflict and peace has made the absence of one imply the existence of the other; the absence of peace implies a conflict, and a transition away from conflict moves towards peace. Richmond and Mitchell (2011) discuss the notion of hybrid forms of peace, or the ways in which societies transitioning from conflict experience peacebuilding through unconventional processes. The edited volume *Hybrid Forms of Peace* discusses agency, resistance, hybridization, and local representations in processes of liberal peacebuilding that enable societies in transition to cultivate peace in situations of conflict, instability, and insecurity.

Undoubtedly, scholarship has examined peace less as a status quo – to understand it as a phenomenon, as a dynamic, or as a characteristic of social order – and more as a prospect and as a desire, making it less tangible and vaguer as a scientific concept. Processed through the framework of conflict resolution more than any other contextual framework, peace has been examined more in its absence and less as an observable event. Galtung's work on peace has addressed this gap to a great extent, by presenting peace as a spectrum and less as an end goal. Within this spectrum, which ranges from negative to positive peace, various degrees of peace can be achieved, and they can be observed and measured in a tangible manner. While negative peace signifies the absence of violence and the coexistence of rival groups, degrees of positive peace incorporate factors of meaningful interaction, cooperation, and social justice that differentiate it from the mere absence of violence (Galtung, 1969).

It comes as no surprise that examining peace implies the scholarly engagement with processes of conflict resolution. Nevertheless, this approach overlooks ways in which societies can foster, redefine, or revisit dynamics of peace – particularly of positive peace and social justice – which occur beyond mechanisms of conflict resolution and peacebuilding. For example, international tourist activity is a social phenomenon of intergroup interaction that can have a direct impact on the interpersonal and intercommunal relationships of people across and within societies. Tourism has been thoroughly discussed in reference to its correlation to peace yet exploring this relationship solely through the conflict resolution route may yield confined results. This chapter seeks to identify indirect routes to peace, and accordingly shed light on the thoroughly addressed correlation between peace and tourism.

DEFINING AND MEASURING PEACE

Galtung's work offered new perspectives in understanding peace by identifying two forms of peace, positive and negative (Galtung, 1969). While negative peace is the mere absence of violence, positive peace is the societal state that is free of both physical and structural violence and can effectively embrace equity and social justice. Anderson (2004) highlights the importance of making peace a measurable and tangible concept and defines peace by differentiating between objective vs. subjective measures, and micro vs. macro contexts. Farmaki and Stergiou (2021) highlight that there is a direct relationship between peace, development, security, and human rights. Admittedly, peace is a combination of factors that provide a secure and stable setting for people to coexist, cooperate, and create in safety, equality, and justice irrespective of their affiliations and identities.

A prominent approach to calculating peace has been the development of reports and indices that evaluate a society's performance towards the above conditions, and thus its ability to foster and sustain peace for its members. One of the most acknowledged indices on peace is the Global Peace Index (GPI) by the Institute for Economics and Peace (IEP). Comprised of 23 indicators developed and confirmed in 2007, the GPI calculates the level to which violence is absent, therefore measuring a basic form of negative, or cold peace. The 23 indicators applied are shown in Table 4.1.

Despite its thorough research design and comprehensive indicators, the 2022 GPI report acknowledges the subjectivity around the task of measuring peace, and highlights, when referring to the index methodology, that peace is "notoriously difficult to define" (Vision of Humanity, 2022). IEP issues a set of peace-related indices in addition to the GPI, some being state-specific, such as the Mexico Peace Index. Interestingly, IEP issues the Positive Peace Report (PPR) in addition to the GPI, to measure peace beyond the absence of violence, through established societal structures and institutions that can protect it. The eight factors considered in the PPR are: (1) a well-functioning government, (2) low levels of corruption, (3) a sound business environment, (4) equitable distribution of resources, (5) acceptance of the rights of others, (6) free flow of information, (7) high levels of human capital, and (8) good relations with neighbours (ibid.). According to the 2022 report, seven out of the eight factors considered have been improved on an average global scale, except for the factor of corruption, which deteriorated. Overall, the PPR shows records of increased positive peace globally over the past decade. A comparison between the GPI indicators and the PPR factors is illustrated in Table 4.1, indicating how the concepts of negative and positive peace apply distinct approaches to measuring peace.

Table 4.1   *Measuring negative and positive peace*

Negative Peace Indicators			Positive Peace Factors
Ongoing Domestic and International Conflict	Societal Safety and Security	Militarization	
1. Number and duration of internal conflicts	7. Level of perceived criminality in society	18. Military expenditure as a percentage of GDP	1. Well-functioning government
2. Number of deaths from external organized conflict	8. Number of refugees and internally displaced people as a percentage of the population	19. Number of armed services personnel per 100,000 people	2. Low levels of corruption
3. Number of deaths from internal organized conflict	9. Political instability	20. Volume of transfers of major conventional weapons as recipient (imports) per 100,000 people	3. Sound business environment
4. Number, duration, and role of external conflicts	10. Political Terror Scale	21. Volume of transfers of major conventional weapons as supplier (exports) per 100,000 people	4. Equitable distribution of resources
5. Intensity of organized internal conflict	11. Impact of terrorism	22. Financial contribution to UN peacekeeping missions	5. Acceptance of the rights of others
6. Relations with neighbouring countries	12. Number of homicides per 100,000 people	23. Nuclear and heavy weapons capabilities	6. Free flow of information
	13. Level of violent crime		7. High levels of human capital
	14. Violent demonstrations		8. Good relations with neighbours
	15. Number of jailed population per 100,000 people		

	Negative Peace Indicators		Positive Peace Factors
Ongoing Domestic and International Conflict	Societal Safety and Security	Militarization	
	16. Number of internal security officers and police per 100,000 people		
	17. Ease of access to small arms and light weapons		

Source: Author (adapted from the Global Peace Index 2022 report, Vision of Humanity).

According to McConaghy (2012), the GPI has ranked states according to their peacefulness, a factor that directly informs of a society's resilience and ability to flourish. The 23 GPI indicators make peace tangible and measurable despite its intuitive and subjective character (ibid.). At the same time, the eight positive peace factors identified provide the framework for the structural attributes of peaceful, and thus resilient and flourishing societies (ibid.).

Pratt and Liu (2016) chose the GPI rankings to discuss a country's level of peace in reference to tourism and tourist arrivals to that country, in their examination of the tourism and peace relationship. Their approach quantifies the relationship between tourism and peace by associating international tourist arrivals with the destination's GPI scores. Pratt and Liu's examination is one that establishes a direct correlation between non-violent societies and increased tourist activity, but it does not confirm any relationship of causation between the two examined variables. Moreover, the study's focus on negative or cold peace indicators allows for an evaluation of tourist arrivals in the absence of violence – or fear of violence – and does not incorporate components of peace that make it reflective of sustainable and resilient societies. To this end, considering the GPI as an indicator of a lack of violence in combination with factors of positive peace would provide a more comprehensive assessment of a country's structural and systemic levels of peacefulness.

The evident distinction between negative and positive peace is acknowledged in the GPI report, which calculates a country's disparity between its GPI and PPR scores and presents this calculation as the *positive peace deficit*. Countries with the highest positive peace deficit include, for the 2022 calculations, Equatorial Guinea, Timor-Leste, Djibouti, and Rwanda. The positive peace deficit is a fundamental component of the GPI, because it serves as a predictor of violence. Another noteworthy observation derived from the GPI is that Cyprus, a country experiencing a decades-long intractable conflict, has received high ranks in GPI metrics, and is placed in the "High State of Peace" category with a score of 1,903. Although this indicates a low risk of violence,

Cyprus is also calculated to have had an economic cost due to its unresolved conflict. Cyprus' quest for peace is discussed in more detail in this chapter's following sections, with specific reference to international peacebuilding initiatives on the island.

Another set of indicators measuring peace comes from the United Nations and the Sustainable Development Goals framework. Goal 16, which refers to achieving Peace, Justice and Strong Institutions, is assessed through a set of ten targets and 24 indicators, covering access to citizenship, voting, human rights institutions, transparency, and inclusive decision-making. According to Kornioti and Antoniou (2022), the ten targets formulated for reaching Sustainable Development Goal 16 (SDG 16) address five primary thematic areas: (1) violence (targets 1 and 2), (2) justice, corruption, and crime (targets 3, 4, 5, and 9), (3) inclusive and participatory decision-making (target 7), (4) strong local and global institutions (targets 7 and 8), and (5) fundamental freedoms (target 10). Although not identical, some of the SGD 16 indicators reflect indicators of the GPI and factors of the PPR, including violence, conflict, corruption, and access to information. Criticism of SDG 16 highlights that the goal needs to further develop its capacity to measure peace, with the current targets and indicators lacking the ability to do so adequately, particularly for the African continent (Bolaji-Adio, 2015). Despite its lack of a comprehensive measurement approach and its low level of institutionalization, SDG 16 manages to offer a moral reference and an "international ethical norm" for peace that can be further quantified and institutionalized in the future (Ivanovic et al., 2018: 49).

The Role of Tourism

The correlation between tourism and peace has intrigued researchers for decades, who have attempted to confirm whether tourism can be a causal factor to peace, or whether peace is a condition that encourages tourism. D'Amore (1988: 269) advocated for the ability of tourism to act as a force for peace and suggested that tourism enables the world to envision a "positive concept of peace" by experiencing the exchange of ideas and best practices. In a more recent account, Blanchard and Higgins-Desbiolles (2013) present peace as a multidimensional social concept encompassing justice, human rights, and sustainability, presenting tourism as a force that prevents war from unfolding, acting as a protective shield over formerly attained peace.

Conversely, Ap and Var's (1990: 267) quantitative findings indicated that the positive social impact deriving from tourist activity is not substantive for tourism to be viewed as a "significant contributor to world peace". Instead, it should be considered merely as an economic activity with positive outcomes. Farmaki and Stergiou (2021) add to the criticism of tourism as a contributor to peace and say that tourist activity is considered to reinforce inequalities on the economic, political, and socio-cultural front.

Moufakkir and Kelly (2010) advocate that there is a role for tourism to play in establishing peace, especially since tourism is a major platform for intercultural contact. Nevertheless, there are various obstacles to be resolved before tourism can generate meaningful impact to encourage global peace. Addressing these obstacles requires a purposeful differentiation between tourist activities that enhance and that hinder peace. This responsibility lies across actors in tourism, from state governments to the individual traveller (ibid.).

Farmaki (2017) identifies four facets that tourism comprises of: the economic, the political, the social, and the environmental. Acknowledging all four facets is key in understanding tourism's transformative assets, rather than to define it solely as an economic activity. Farmaki proceeds to assess the reconciliation potential of tourism and establish a model for the peace-through-tourism argument by differentiating the ways in which tourism informs the conflict to peace continuum. Distinguishing between active and passive forms of tourist behaviour, tourism can either be an inhibitor of peace – in its passive forms – a subservient or moderator of positive peace, or a mediator through more active tourist behaviour (ibid.). In both its subservient and mediating capacities, certain forms of tourism can have a direct impact on enhancing intergroup relations, promoting transformative learning, and establishing direct contributions to reconciliatory efforts. Providing an encouraging environment for tourism to facilitate educative and transformational experiences is, therefore, critical for achieving meaningful tourism-led reconciliation and peace.

Farmaki (2022) further delves into the relationship between tourism and peace to identify external determinants to the tourism and peace relationship, including factors such as governmental support, international organization support, and the willingness between rival groups to embrace peace and reconcile. Tourism's potential to encourage positive exchanges between members of adversary communities and engage hosts and visitors in transformational and educative experiences makes tourism a vehicle for peace and reconciliation, and a tool that can be employed purposefully in post-conflict and peacebuilding settings (ibid.). The role of tourism in encouraging peace through processes of conflict resolution is further discussed below.

PEACE THROUGH CONFLICT RESOLUTION

The practice of conflict resolution takes place at three distinct levels: the military one, the political one, and the civil society/grassroots one. Ramsbotham and Woodhouse (1999) present a conflict's stages from escalation to resolution through three phases: conflict containment, conflict settlement, and conflict transformation. Conflict containment refers to the containment of armed violence, and as such refers to the military level of a conflict. At the same time, conflict settlement aims to develop a peace settlement across the political representatives of each party involved in the conflict, making the conflict settlement stage relevant on a political level. Conflict transformation incorporates a social character and addresses the ability of the people to recover from the conflict and reconcile through a transformation of everyday interactions. Conflict transformation therefore applies at the civil society/grassroots level.

Ramsbotham and Woodhouse (1999) illustrate the conflict stages through the Hourglass model, indicating that each stage in the conflict cycle can be addressed by a respective conflict resolution mechanism: conflict containment is addressed through war limitation and peacekeeping mechanisms, conflict settlement through peacemaking, and conflict transformation through peacebuilding. According to Galtung (1969) peacekeeping, peacemaking, and peacebuilding are the three angles of the peace triangle model that he employs to illustrate a comprehensive framework of conflict resolution intervention.

Table 4.2 illustrates a comprehensive approach to conflict resolution.

Table 4.2   Levels of conflict resolution

Conflict Stage	Level	Conflict Resolution Mechanism
Conflict Containment	Military	Peacekeeping
Conflict Settlement	Political	Peacemaking
Conflict Transformation	Civil society/Grassroots	Peacebuilding

Source: Author (informed by Galtung, 1969; Ramsbotham and Woodhouse, 1999).

On the military level, Fortna (2008) identifies three consent-based types of peacekeeping missions, which occur with the approval of the parties in conflict: (1) the observational missions, that carry out monitoring operations by either military or civilian observers, (2) the interpositional missions, in which monitoring is conducted by lightly armed troops, and (3) the multidimensional missions, involving both military and civilians that offer complementary services to the smooth implementation of a peace settlement at the political level. A prominent example of peacekeeping missions is the work done by the peacekeeping forces of the United Nations. An additional means of peacekeeping is operations of peace enforcement, which refer to third-party interventions that occur without the consent of the parties in conflict.

On the political level, peacemaking processes address a conflict's political settlement, oftentimes through mediated negotiations or third-party intervention involving Track One leaders, with the aim of establishing state-building processes for a period of political and constitutional transition away from escalated conflict. The end goal of peacemaking processes is a political settle-ment that formally reinstates peace across the formerly rival parties (Fisher, 1997). Zartman (2007) defines third party assistance in processes of conflict settlement as the diplomatic efforts taken to resolve a conflict.

Peacebuilding interventions address the stage of conflict transformation and engage civil society and individual citizens in a transition towards peaceful, sustainable, and positive coexistence. Fisher (1993) considers peacebuilding efforts as a vital step for making processes of developing a political settle-ment viable, by engaging the members of communities in conflict with the idea of reconciliation with former enemies. Developing a peace settlement on the political without addressing the public's needs and concerns through transitional reconciliation could directly hinder the implementation of that settlement and lead the conflict back to escalation.

Tourism, Conflict, and Peace

Much of the discussion on the correlation between tourism and peace through conflict resolution has been about the role tourism has played throughout a conflict's discourse and how it has informed processes of post-conflict tran-sition and reconciliation. In the case of reinstating peace in post-conflict soci-eties, tourism can be seen both as an indicator of restored safety and security in the post-conflict destination, as well as an indicator of improved relations between former rivals (Anastasopoulos, 1992; Bar-Tal and Bennick, 2004).

In its diversity of forms, tourism has been taking place both despite a con-flict's occurrence, but also because of it. In the former case, conventional forms of tourist activity and short-term travel, such as recreational or business tourism, take place in destinations that have experienced conflict, but can provide sufficient safety to travellers who wish to complete their priorly planned journeys. In the latter case, a society experiencing conflict may attract visitors that wish to directly experience the ongoing dispute, whether out of recreational curiosity, or for professional reasons.

Conflict-oriented travel has been conceptualized under the umbrella of dark tourism, a phenomenon coined in the late twentieth century to highlight an overlooked incentive within the realm of international travel: the fascination over the portrayal of morbid phenomena and the exploration of the physical remnants of a past tragedy (Foley and Lennon, 1996; Seaton, 1996; Lennon and Foley, 2000; Stone, 2006; Sharpley and Stone, 2009). Like other forms of special interest tourist activity in the post-Fordist era and beyond, authenticity is a key part of the dark tourist experience, manifesting through the trigger of the senses, the ambience, and the site's intensities (Trauer, 2006). A site with an authentic display of its macabre past or morbid present can be identified as a dark tourism destination, with popular examples being the Alcatraz prisons, the site of the Auschwitz Concentration Camp, the 9/11 Memorial site in Manhattan, New York, as well as active war zones, locations of former battle-fields, and cemeteries. Additional examples falling within the dark site realm can be artistic representations or staged settings that entail morbid and macabre elements, such as skeletons or decaying post-mortal human bodies.

According to Stone and Sharpley, elements of tragedy, suffering, death, and decay are the main indicators of a site's "darkness" (Stone, 2005; Stone and Sharpley, 2008) while Biran and Poria (2012) add violence and risk to these indicators. Visiting a dark site may entail an educational component (Cohen, 2011), or can be an emotional experience (Podoshen, 2013), especially in cases where elements of the destination are perceived as heritage or the destination is associated with a community's history (Biran et al., 2011). For conflict and post-conflict destinations, the dark element is derived from the tragedy of the conflict's occurrence and its often-devastating outcomes, including death, division, and displacement. The conflict's remnants and physical man-ifestations become a form of dissonant, or dark, heritage, and are featured as a component of the destination's local character and identity.

Dark tourism, which has been interpreted as an experience of "deviant leisure" and an opportunity for "social passage", is gaining popularity glob-ally and is increasingly becoming more diverse (Stone and Sharpley, 2013). Nevertheless, it remains, unsurprisingly, a controversial form of tourist activ-ity; the profiling of a destination with a focus on its dark history has often met strong opposition, especially amongst local communities that consider such profiling misleading and disrespectful (Lennon and Foley, 2000). An evident oxymoron is that, although local populations at a destination with a dark affiliation might associate with the dark element negatively, the intrigue of exploring this dark element may assume a positive association for the foreign visitor. According to Stone and Sharpley (2008: 585), "dark tourism allows the re-conceptualization of death and mortality into forms that stimulate something other than primordial terror and dread", a dynamic that makes it inevitable for a tourist–host clash to occur.

There is a distinction to be made between *conflict-oriented* and *peace-oriented* forms of tourism. The former refers to the macabre fascination of experiencing a conflict's authenticity – either while it unfolds or by encountering its after-math – whereas the latter is driven by an interest in conflict resolution and the prospects of establishing peace in a conflict-ridden destination.

There are two principal forms of peace-oriented tourism: *peace tourism* and *peacebuilding tourism*. Peace tourism refers to the general inclination towards examining a destination's relationship with peace and its prospects for peace-fulness in the future. The tourist's motivation is driven by an interest in peace dynamics, transitional processes towards peace, or a current state of peace in a destination that experienced severe conflict or division in the past. This

peace-oriented motivation can cover a vast range of preferences and expectations, from personal curiosity to professional contributions to the destination's
peace status. Peace tourism can occur either from a community-oriented
or from a self-oriented standpoint (Antoniou, 2022a). In the former case,
the tourist experience is shaped by the desire to contribute to peace for the
destination visited, ideally in ways that complement existing international or
community-based efforts. In the latter case, a self-oriented standpoint would
prioritize the tourist's personal development and self-enhancement over
impacts to the community. The self-oriented peace tourist may have a passive
engagement with the visited communities and yield negligible outputs. At
the same time, however, there is considerable likelihood of unintentionally
generating negative outcomes for the host communities through host–visitor
controversies (ibid.).

Peace tourism can be further divided into recreational vs professionally
motivated forms (Antoniou, 2022b). The second category that distinguishes the
professional capacity through which tourists engage in peace-oriented travel
has been specifically identified as peacebuilding tourism (ibid.). Although it
is a form of niche tourism that is characterized by the tourist's professional
ability to identify, evaluate, and contribute to a destination's prospects of
peace, it can still achieve various levels of impact for the destination. The
peacebuilding tourist can engage in a destination's peace dynamics on an
intentional level, coincidentally, or as a benign peacebuilding tourist, yielding
negligible to no impact.

It is often challenging to engage in the construction and promotion of
peace in a destination transitioning from conflict without focusing on the
occurrence of conflict as well and the factors that brought about tensions
among the members of the host communities. There are, therefore, blurry
lines when attempting to distinguish where conflict-oriented tourism stops and
where peace-oriented tourism begins. A factor, however, that makes forms of
peace-oriented tourism stand out is the intention to identify patterns of peacefulness in the destination visited, to envision how peace can be strengthened,
and – where possible – to assist and support it.

Tourism can be employed in the pursuit of peace in settings of conflict
transformation, and this pursuit can take place through multiple avenues.
Carbone and Oosterbeek (2021) suggest that one such avenue is offered
through cultural heritage management, which can create direct links between
tourism and peace. Jamgade (2021) points to tourism's significance in achieving sustainable peacebuilding, and Farmaki and Stergiou (2021) recommend
exploring the contribution of tourism to peace as an instrument of social
justice. Sustainability and resilience are recurring themes in the discussion
of tourism and peace (Aulet and Tarrés, 2021; Farmaki and Stergiou, 2021;

Jamgade, 2021); themes that are examined in more detail in the section on sustainable development below.

PEACE THROUGH SUSTAINABLE DEVELOPMENT

Peace and international development have a longstanding relationship of correlation and mutual causation. Peace is considered to enable and advance development, while development, prosperity, and welfare are catalytic in sustaining and preserving peaceful coexistence within and across communities. The Sustainable Development agenda set forth by the UN through 17 goals sets peace as one of these goals, advocating that one of the key avenues for achieving sustainable development is through peace, justice, and strong institutions.

According to Farmaki and Stergiou (2021), tourism can be a reparative and preventive tool in fostering sustainable peace if considered as an agent of justice. Tourism can be more comprehensively understood as a tool in peacebuilding if it is examined in reference to how it impacts global inequalities and injustices. Identifying the ways in which international tourist activity can contribute to equality and a spread of cosmopolitan values to contribute to sustainable development – and thus to sustainable peace – was also a central theme in Chapter 1 on "Tourism and international development".

The United Nations has actively pursued development through peace not only in the case of the SDG agenda, but also by making peacebuilding a central component of its principal development agency, the United Nations Development Programme (UNDP). UNDP's work focuses on three interconnected areas: sustainable development, democratic governance and peacebuilding, and climate and disaster resilience; the agency's mission to "help people build a better life" is pursued through efforts to establish peacefulness and make it sustainable to achieve community resilience (UNDP, 2022). Examples of peacebuilding interventions undertaken by UNDP include the UNDP-ACT project that was implemented in Cyprus between 2005 and 2015 (UNDP, 2015), as well as the country Programme Development project for Libya, which is planned to be implemented between 2023 and 2025 and focus on sustainable growth and peacebuilding (UNDP Libya, 2022). UNDP's work reaffirms that achieving peace and development are two interrelated and interdependent objectives.

A report issued on the first years of UNDP-ACT's operations – 2005–2008 – highlights the thematic areas addressed by ACT's peacebuilding projects and explains how each initiative under ACT contributed to peacebuilding in Cyprus (UNDP-ACT, 2008). The thematic areas incorporate work on social inclusion, cultural understanding, the environment, and health, while some of these projects address specific audiences from the divided communities: examples of niche audiences targeted include youth, filmmakers, and journalists. In response to how each initiative achieves peacebuilding in Cyprus, the project on the environment reads:

> It is obvious from the work of UNEP and others around the world that the Environment is an ideal conflict resolution tool. This is very true in Cyprus, where on a small island, environmental priorities are identical in both communities, and problems such as pest control, viral pandemics, and air pollution cannot be contained by the buffer zone. The Cyprus Environmental Stakeholder Forum (CESF) is an unprecedented effort by the environmental community in Cyprus to speak with a common voice. (UNDP-ACT, 2008: 11)

Jarraud and Lordos (2012) use the example of UNDP-ACT's peacebuilding engagement through environmental work to discuss the notion of environmental conflict resolution. They suggest that, like the report above suggests, the environment provides an effective peacebuilding tool, and it can be used as an entry point to conflict resolution work that involves citizen participation. Ironically, although UNDP's 2008 report highlights pandemics as a problem to be addressed jointly by the partitioned communities of Cyprus, the response to the COVID-19 pandemic in 2020 was to halt any form of intercommunal movement across the island's UN-administered Buffer Zone that separates the Greek and Turkish Cypriot communities. The restrictions in trans-communal movement were announced by the authorities of both communities as a measure to limit the spread of the virus, and were restored several months later in the summer of 2021, when the pandemic appeared to be under control.

In 2009, UNDP-ACT launched the Economic Interdependence Project involving the chambers of commerce from the island's two partitioned communities (Apostolides et al., 2012). The project's aim was to examine areas of economic interdependence between the Greek and Turkish Cypriot communities of Cyprus, to foster inter-communal business partnerships, and to draft a joint economic development plan (ibid.). Until its completion in 2015, UNDP-ACT implemented a series of peacebuilding projects that focused on empowering members of the local communities to work together and envision a common future. In doing so, ACT projects and initiatives occurred in reference to areas of sustainable development, addressing the three pillars of sustainable development – environmental conservation, social welfare, and economic progress – as well as additional areas of focus such as cultural heritage, gender, and youth.

Interestingly, the work of UNDP in Cyprus through the UNDP-ACT project has delivered noteworthy contributions to the examination and measurement of peace within and beyond Cyprus. One of the local organizations that were beneficiaries of the UNDP-ACT funding scheme, the Centre for Sustainable Peace and Democratic Development (SeeD), developed a new index that measured

peace through indicators of social cohesion and reconciliation. More specifically, the Social Cohesion and Reconciliation (SCORE) Index is "a smart and
versatile assessment tool designed to measure different components of social
cohesion as well as resilience capacities and vulnerability factors around the
world in order to inform the efforts of peacebuilding and development actors
with robust and scientific evidence" (SCORE, 2022).

The index was first employed in the Cypriot context to produce the first
SCORE report in 2015 (SCORE, 2015), and has since then expanded to calculate the SCORE of ten countries – including updated metrics for Cyprus.
These countries are Liberia, Nepal, Bosnia-Herzegovina, Moldova, Malaysia,
Armenia, South Sudan, Ivory Coast, and Ukraine – with a separate SCORE
also calculated for Eastern Ukraine. The methodology behind SCORE is
informed through a content framework, a process framework, and an analytical
tool. The index is designed around five indicators that are considered the main
determinants of a society's exposure to positive peace and resilience against
change, as well as indicators of individual and group wellbeing: these are (1)
human security, (2) human capability, (3) meaningful civic participation and
engagement, (4) community cohesion and harmonious intergroup relations,
and (5) institutional and economic development. The SCORE Index design
reaffirms that notions of security, development, social cohesion, and sustainability are interlinked, solidifying the interconnectedness between sustainable
development and peace, but also reinforcing the tangible nature of peace,
through an ability to first measure it, then assess it across destinations, and
finally pursue it, through its key determinants.

The case study of UNDP-ACT in Cyprus does not only allow for direct links
to be made between peace and sustainable development, but also provides
insights as to how tourism has played a role in the ACT's implementation.
Findings from the programme's later stages show that the dichotomy between
international and local peacebuilders did not effectively capture the range
of stakeholders involved in ACT (Antoniou, 2021). One overlooked agent
was the programme's visiting peacebuilding professionals, or peacebuilding
tourists (ibid.). In their capacity as external consultants, experts, or individual
professionals interested in the peacebuilding discourse in Cyprus, visiting
peacebuilders contributed positively to the project's peace-oriented initiatives
and were well-received by local peacebuilder audiences (ibid.). Findings
from Cyprus's UNDP-ACT project and the island's peacebuilding discourse
more broadly suggest that international peacebuilding agencies can work
more effectively with local peacebuilders through a more active and direct
engagement of peacebuilding tourist audiences (ibid.). The tourist capacity of
peacebuilding professionals was also employed in the data collection process
for calculating the SCORE Index across ten countries. Developed initially
under the auspices of UNDP-ACT, the initiative for implementing the SCORE

index to a number of conflict-ridden destinations applied the peacebuilder paradigm of a tri-party collaboration between representatives of international peacebuilding institutions, short-term visiting peacebuilding professionals, and local stakeholders (Antoniou, 2021).

PEACE THROUGH DIPLOMACY

Diplomacy has hitherto been acknowledged as the art of negotiation among state actors and their representatives. Interstate negotiations and multilateral state diplomacy have paved the way for peace settlements, ceasefire agreements, memorandums, and frameworks for collaboration, formally establishing meaningful collaboration between the actors involved.

State diplomacy has been a principal form of conflict settlement and a key process for establishing a conflict's political and constitutional resolution. The United Nations is a principal international actor offering third-party intervention for conflict settlement, such as mediated negotiations between actors in conflict. Nevertheless, when diplomacy's contribution to peace is examined through processes of conflict resolution, the results are not encouraging. Peace settlements between state actors often take extended periods to achieve, and at times diplomatic efforts reach dead ends; in the case of active conflicts, a dead end can lead to intractability, leaving the conflict unsettled, whereas in a different scenario, diplomatic efforts among states may leave key non-state actors out of the negotiating table.

Despite the observations in conflict resolution processes, diplomacy has been a prominent tool in establishing multilateral and transnational frameworks of peaceful coexistence. The establishment of the Sustainable Development Goals agenda as a transnational reference point of sustainable development for the member states of the United Nations is the result of multilateral state diplomacy. The SDG framework specifically includes SDG 16 on Peace, Justice, and Strong Institutions, and provides internationally accepted indicators for measuring and evaluating peace.

Diplomacy has been employed as a tool not only for resolving, but also for preventing conflict among states and thus protecting their peaceful coexistence. This approach was specifically applied to coordinate the transnational governance of shared water resources, an initiative that has been measured through the Blue Peace Index. Developed by the Economist Intelligence Unit, the Blue Peace Index employs five pillars to measure the effectiveness of shared water resource management across states. Through the pillars of (1) policy and legal frameworks, (2) institutional arrangement and participation, (3) water management instruments, (4) infrastructure and financing, and (5) cooperation, the index assesses the level to which states sharing a common water basin coordinate and collaborate over its distribution, to avoid scenarios of water scarcity and to eliminate the possibility of resource-oriented conflicts (Economist Impact, 2022). The Blue Peace Index records, which currently account for interstate collaboration across seven river basins, indicate the Sava River as a best practice example for the collaboration and water management practices employed by Croatia, Serbia, Slovenia, and Bosnia-Herzegovina. The lowest score is calculated for the Tigris-Euphrates River affecting Iran, Iraq, Turkey, and Syria. The profound lack of collaboration among the policy-makers involved has led to a severely challenged management practice of the river basin, which currently relies on ad-hoc measures that fail to effectively address water allocation and pollution control.

Beyond state diplomacy, cosmopolitan diplomacy is a promising avenue for non-state actors to engage in international negotiations and develop coordinated action on global causes and challenges. Cosmopolitan diplomacy is particularly relevant for understanding tourism's contribution to peace, since it is the form of diplomacy that can engage international political actors for global causes and embrace the input of unconventional non-state actors. The tourist as an active citizen has the capacity to perform political acts and, through niche interaction with members of a destination, to examine, negotiate, and act on peace. In the case of challenges that transcend national borders such as environmental crises, water management issues, and resource allocation efficiency, the failure of interstate collaboration can be revisited through channels of global civil society and cosmopolitan political activism that would be enabled through travel. The Tigris Euphrates and the Amu Darya examples that score the lowest on the Blue Peace Index on water management collaboration are crucial global challenges with security risks of regional and international magnitude. There is, therefore, a role for non-state actors to play and, through cosmopolitan platforms and global civil society mobilization, individuals and organized groups to establish alternatives to state misman-agement and lack of cooperation. Another avenue that would be considered unconventional for existing state diplomacy practices would be to establish platforms of diplomatic exchange across individual citizens whose lives are affected by poor state collaboration, and whose resources are mismanaged. Diplomatic avenues for citizens and tourists as non-state political contributors could not only create escape routes from state-level diplomacy when it reaches dead ends. Cosmopolitan forms of citizen diplomacy would also provide a significantly more inclusive, democratic, and comprehensive diplomatic exchange with expectedly more applicable, commonly acceptable, and thus sustainable outcomes.

As discussed in the relationship between tourism, peace, and sustainable development, the environment plays a critical role in engaging communities in conflict with peacebuilding through a common cause. Efforts for environmen-tal protection and measures against climate change have engaged states, civil society, and individual citizens to mobilize transnationally and work together, achieving environmental progress and peaceful coexistence at the same time. Cosmopolitan diplomacy has the capacity to incorporate the plethora of actors engaged in environmental work and activism and start inclusive discussions on environmental action on a global scale. Peace and peacebuilding tourists can engage in environmental conflict resolution through their short-term travel and apply diplomacy in an inclusive, non-formal way to engage rival communities in the cause of environmental protection. Through the environmental perspective, development and diplomacy offer new and interconnected pathways to achieving sustainable peace, and provide tourists, whether peace tourists, peacebuilding tourists, or cosmopolitan tourist diplomats, with the opportunity to actively engage in these processes.

PEACE THROUGH INTERNATIONAL SECURITY

Chapter 3 discussed the relationship between tourism and international security and revealed that tourist activity can be a source of environmental insecurity. With tourism consumption performed in a carbon-intensive manner and through patterns of an unsustainable exploitation of recourses, international tourist activity has challenged perceptions of environmental security and sustainability, particularly for fragile destinations.

Looking at international security through Buzan et al.'s (1998) five security sectors, Chapter 3 revealed that tourism generates substantial influence in all five sectors. While the military, political, and societal sectors can benefit from the contributions of tourism and the activity's growing international influence, the economic and environmental sectors are burdened by the patterns of tourism production and consumption that are applied today. Heightened levels of insecurity in either the economic or the environmental sectors can directly threaten peace and elevate the risk of violence or fear of violence. Nevertheless, as the UNDP-ACT example shows, both the economic and the environmental sector can be utilized as avenues for peacebuilding, with the direct involvement of tourist audiences. For the environmental sector in particular, the notion of environmental conflict resolution could open new pathways to peace simply by connecting like-minded individuals aspiring to shift patterns of environmental degradation. Tourism is, therefore, a practice that has the capacity to both eliminate phenomena of international insecurity, as well as enhance security and peace on a global scale.

Part of what makes tourism a catalyst in global socio-political affairs is, in addition to its ability to bring about positive socio-political change, the realization that some forms of tourism pose a threat to global causes and cosmopolitan values. Distinguishing between forms of tourist activity that can foster positive global change and those that restrict it is a key step towards establishing a targeted and informed global tourism impact. Tourism's significant role in achieving or undermining international security in the environmental sector indicates the capacity tourism holds as a form of International Relations.

PEACE THROUGH TOURISM REVISITED

There is an evident need for any scholarly attempt to unlock the tourism and peace relationship to first ask: which form of tourist activity and tourist behaviour is being assessed? The wide scope of international tourism makes it unrealistic to establish a simplistic bilateral correlation between tourism as a unitary phenomenon and peace as a straightforward objective. From Farmaki's (2017) perspective that tourism occurs through four separate facets and in both active and passive forms, to the multiple indices measuring peace through a diversity of indicator combinations, both tourism and peace need to be further specified before evaluating their association. Figure 4.1 tries to encapsulate how, before identifying a tourist activity and measuring its contribution to certain aspects of peace, a key distinction ought to be made between unsustainable trends of passive tourist activity and tourism that is driven by cosmopolitan values and can lead to community-oriented contributions that will benefit a host destination. This distinction is illustrated in the spectrum of tourist activity below, and it is a key step in identifying the forms of tourism that merely indicate peace – at its various levels from negative to positive – and the forms of tourism that can contribute to peace, build it, and strengthen it further.

Source: Author (informed by Farmaki, 2017).

Figure 4.1   The tourist as a contributor to peace

At the passive end of the spectrum in Figure 4.1, one can find tourists with more self-oriented leisure objectives that can be satisfied through patterns of familiarity and perceived safety. At this end of the spectrum, it is more likely to find mass tourists and travellers wishing to experience tourist zones and franchised infrastructure to achieve low levels of novelty. The search for familiarity also affects the levels of cross-cultural and intergroup communication, which are expectedly low, leading to low likelihood for the tourist experience to be transformative either for the host community or the tourists themselves. At the same time, the passive forms of tourist activity are expected to be encouraged by a sense of security and stability, and therefore they can be treated as informative indicators of the lack of violence or fear of violence (negative peace). At the extreme end of the passive side of the spectrum lies the mass tourist, as an example of a passive tourist that engages in a packaged vacation that is externally prepared in bulk and, if no measures for economic, societal, or environmental sustainability are taken by the agencies and suppliers providing the mass tourism packages, the tourist will have limited flexibility in engaging with the destination in a sustainable and conscious manner. A key characteristic of the mass tourist category is that it demonstrates significant reliance on tourist-oriented infrastructure, transportation, products, and services, particularly when consuming all-inclusive holiday packages.

Moving further right across the spectrum, forms of tourist activity are more likely to escape their passive engagement with the destination visited and perform coincidental forms of citizen diplomacy, educational peace tourism experiences, and activities that enable more frequent interactions with members of the local communities, escaping tourist-designated zones. The active end of the spectrum features an intentional engagement with local communities from an experiential perspective that incorporates multiple aspects of the locally-performed culture – culinary tastes and habits, language and expression patterns, local choices for entertainment and leisure time, local engagement with the outdoors, and local practices in encountering the destination's landscapes and temperatures. This exposure to locality through cosmopolitan forms of active, experiential tourism is bound to contribute to the cross-cultural literacy of the tourist – and even of the hosts – while it also exposes the tourists to the everyday challenges locals face, whether economic, environmental, political, or societal. As the tourist grasps local dynamics through organic processes of genuine local exchanges beyond the formalities of international peacebuilding projects and labels of foreign state representation, the tourist's contributions to the host community's welfare can assume approaches that are vastly different to state or supranational intervention. Forms of active cosmopolitan tourism – or critical cosmopolitan tourism as the last category of tourist activity this spectrum features – include activities of intentional cosmopolitan diplomacy, peacebuilding tourism, environmental activism, host community empowerment, and engagement with initiatives for sustainable development. The critical cosmopolitan tourist lies at the opposite end of the mass tourist category and articulates the ways in which the two tourist categories can entail contradictory philosophies, motivations, and actions. The critical cosmopolitan tourist category expands the spectrum of tourist typologies further, which was often portrayed through the tourist vs. traveller distinction, or the mass tourist vs. the special interest tourist – or the niche tourist. Expanding the spectrum to highlight the tourist category that is expected to contribute the most to peace is vital, not only for the scholarly examination of peace, but also for achieving a comprehensive reconceptualization of how tourism can inform the broader practice of international relations.

The differentiation between tourism as an indicator and tourism as a contributor to peace is established around a fundamental characteristic of tourist activity: cosmopolitanism. The cosmopolitan underpinning of tourist motivation and planning suggests the likelihood in which the tourist is expected to engage with the host community and formulate their consumption practices accordingly. Cosmopolitan-informed tourists have an expectedly higher likelihood for direct and meaningful interaction with members of the communities visited, and their consumption practices are expected to unfold in ways that will support rather than undermine local societal needs and environmental capacities. Tourists who engage with cosmopolitan values from a critical angle are also expected to identify patterns of inequalities, exclusion, and social injustice more readily, and in response encourage the empowerment, agency, and emancipation of the local population, particularly for its marginalized members.

As indicated in Chapter 1, tourist typologies are an enlightening indicator as to which forms of tourism are more active and which are more passive. Active forms of tourism tend to share a set of characteristics that include a fondness for novelty, the desire to avoid mass tourism and tourist-oriented infrastructure, and a motivation to explore and experience for purposes of cross-cultural literacy. These characteristics complement the attributes of critical approaches to tourism, which equip the tourist with the potential to intentionally contribute to a destination's peace and stability – whether by positively contributing to a post-conflict transition, or by supporting dynamics that prevent conflicts from escalating. A critical approach to cosmopolitanism through tourism would take place through a host–visitor interaction that would be characterized by reciprocal communication, balanced power dynamics, and meaningful dialogue.

CONCLUSION

When looking at how tourism can be a contributor to peace, the question to ask is *what types of tourist activity can significantly foster a destination's roadmap towards sustainable peace?* To differentiate between conflict-oriented, peace-oriented, and other forms of tourism in destinations pursuing peace after conflict can be a challenging task. It is, however, an important distinction to make before any attempt to highlight intention and travel motivation, and as such inform the capacity of the tourist to directly become a contributor to peace.

Peace tourism and peacebuilding tourism are direct routes through which the tourist can engage in both educational and professional activities that engage with the potential of a destination to smoothly transition towards positive forms of peacefulness, and, through conflict resolution tools and mechanisms, to contribute to sustainable peace for the host population.

It is equally important to look beyond processes of conflict resolution to define the relationship between tourism and peace from a multiplicity of per-spectives, including diplomacy, development, and security. Studying tourism as an international political activity has shown that its contribution can be cata-lytic to economic progress, social welfare, security, and community resilience. Through this realization, tourism forms a direct relationship with a destina-tion's levels of peacefulness and resilience, which is directly informed by the absence of violence (security), its prospects of international and transnational collaborations (diplomacy), and its ability to establish economic progress and societal welfare while maintaining ecological sustainability (development).

Key observations that surface through this chapter's discussion of the relationship between tourism and peace highlight that the tourist who is most likely to contribute to peace is the tourist with a high and intentional engagement with cosmopolitan values. Mass tourists, who tend to be passive observers of a destination, are more reliant on tourist infrastructure than other tourist categories, and less likely to establish meaningful and transformational exchanges with the local community. Mass tourists lie at the opposite extreme of the critical cosmopolitan tourist – rather than the special interest tourist more broadly – who is the active, informed, and conscious traveller and is more likely to engage in transformational and educative experiences that are beneficial to both the tourist and the locals. Critical cosmopolitan tourist activities are expected to increase cross-cultural literacy and cross-cultural understanding through meaningful contact, support healthy and sustainable economic practices that advance the local communities without exceeding the destination's resource boundaries, and promote patterns of local inclusion and representation, improving the destination's capacity for peace and resilience altogether.

A variety of peace-oriented indices have formulated methodologies to make peace more measurable, and therefore allow its assessment over time to become a tangible objective. As the examination of tourism's contribution to peace continues to evolve, it is important for future studies to employ a com-bination of peace-oriented indices to evaluate the empirical contribution of active cosmopolitan tourism through intentional activities to peace in selected destinations. Quantitative approaches to the refined association between cosmopolitan forms of tourism to designated indicators of peace – such as inclusive governance, representation, social justice, and equity – would significantly advance the peace-through-tourism debate, and move beyond tourism's contribution as a passive indicator of peaceful and secure destinations.

Tourism as a Form of International Relations: conclusion

TOURISM AND INTERNATIONAL RELATIONS AS EVOLVING FIELDS

The ability of travellers to access destinations across the world grew steadily and widely during the era of globalization. The end of the Cold War ended the world's polarity under two global superpowers and shifted security dynamics in a way that expanded the right to travel, while providing access to increasingly more countries that were considered politically safe destinations. Unknown and previously inaccessible destinations became within reach and tourists seized the opportunity to access their novelty while ensuring their safety. Rapid technological advancements and an international, capitalist, free market enabled more frequent and affordable travel. The phenomenon of increased tourist demand was soon met by corresponding supply responses, paving the way for tourist-oriented infrastructural development and a rise of tourist zone creation. Tourist zones, or tourist bubbles, emerged across the world to provide a familiar comfort space for visitors and were characterized by the presence of known Western-based franchises offering a standardized set of products and services.

The post-Cold War period has been characterized by a boom in mass tourism production and consumption. In the years that followed, the expansion of international tourist activity continued, although the mass tourism outbreak soon evolved through market segmentation and the emergence of niche tourism trends, characterized by customized tourist experiences guided by the tourist's interests. The industry continued to expand and evolve with the support of technological advancements, introducing social media and online trends as direct influences on tourist motivation. After surviving a global War on Terror, an international financial crisis, and a pandemic, the international tourism industry reintroduces itself today as an international socioeconomic activity with grave momentum and a global actor – of multiple stakeholders – capable of performing and influencing international political activity.

This book examined and discussed the ways in which tourism conducts international relations. The convention that international relations is a practice exclusively performed by states, and that states are the principally recognized political actors of the world stage has been challenged and thoroughly debunked. Additionally, the establishment of a Western-oriented theoretical framework through which international relations is examined has also been revisited to develop the grounds for a global, post-Western IR. International Relations in the 2020s and onwards will undoubtedly look vastly different ontologically and epistemologically compared to the discipline's origins. It will be more holistic, unconventional, and emancipatory. Most importantly, it will become even more interdisciplinary, with input from research areas previously considered irrelevant.

Tourism, a research field of interdisciplinary character that examines transnational movement, exchange of information, and intercultural global trends within a framework of international socio-political and economic activity, is seeking its place within the new IR. To see Tourism as a form of IR means that we can examine, assess, and analyze tourist activity through theoretical and methodological approaches founded within the field of IR. There is a particular challenge in doing so, because as scholarship has identified, International Relations' theories are at present facing a weakness in predicting new phenomena within the realm of international political activity. What this book has attempted to achieve is twofold: first, it revisits tourism within the International Relations field as an example of a new international political activity, and secondly, it has attempted to inform the IR theoretical spectrum in ways that can better examine and attend to forms of non-state political activity, such as tourism.

At its introductory chapter, the book presents five main IR theories as separate lenses for examining Tourism: Realism, Liberalism, the English School, Constructivism, and Critical Theory. Their examination revealed that more state-centric and conventional IR theories, namely Realism and Liberalism, were confined in their ability to assess and evaluate non-state political activity, and thus to understand international tourist activity comprehensively as a transnational political act. At the same time, however, Neorealism's attention to structure and Neoliberalism's focus on international principles in trade and governance enable the two theories to adopt systemic viewpoints of the international political stage. The English School's streams apply both a state-centric lens, as well as a universalist approach to the examination of international politics, which grants the theory with an adaptability towards new political actors. Constructivism, a theoretical perspective that is close to the English School, is even more adaptable towards the introduction of unconventional non-state actors in IR, as it acknowledges the socially constructed nature of the international political stage and its ability to adjust as social norms evolve through time. This book identifies Critical Theory as the IR theory most appropriate to discuss, examine, and evaluate tourists as political agents, due to its emancipatory and inclusive philosophy. Interestingly, Critical Theory, Constructivism, and the English School – as well as Liberalism to a shorter extent – provided notions of universalism, such as Kantian and other forms of cosmopolitanism, that are appropriate for the examination of tourism within the IR field.

A pillar for the effective understanding of Tourism as a form of International Relations has been the contribution of tourist activity to sustainable development. Chapter 1 introduces this relationship and highlights that, despite criticisms on the vagueness of measuring and evaluating sustainable development, the goal of achieving sustainability is neither intangible nor ambiguous. The Sustainable Development Goals provide a comprehensive attempt to break down sustainable development into 17 goals, each with a set of approximately ten measurable indicators. The SDGs have already been employed to calculate the impact of the COVID-19 pandemic on each goal and on sustainable development altogether, identifying significant setbacks on economic and social progress (United Nations, 2022). While critics have also been sceptic about the comprehensiveness and efficacy of the SDGs, there is an evident evolution of efforts for sustainability and conservation from the 1970s onwards, encouraging optimism for growing international capabilities around the effective assessment and delivery of sustainable development. Tourism has the capacity to choose between reinforcing existing, unsustainable practices, or take active steps in reverting its record of unsustainable practice by establishing sustainable production and consumption patterns, empowering local communities to escape models of economic dependency, and directly contributing to informed and meaningful cross-cultural interaction that could progressively increase cultural literacy and combat prejudice.

A key approach to differentiating between conducive and harmful forms of tourist activity comes from the framework of critical cosmopolitanism. To employ cosmopolitan values as a push factor in travel implies that tourist activity is directly informed by an understanding of the world as an interconnected sphere, one where citizenship and ethnic or religious affiliation is not prioritized over humanity. Viewing cosmopolitanism from a critical angle allows tourism to employ cosmopolitan values to deconstruct global hierarchies and inequalities and grant agency to unconventional political actors on a global scale, both hosts and visitors.

Cosmopolitanism is a central theme in Chapter 2 as well, which discusses the relationship between tourism and diplomacy. Viewing international diplomatic activity as a state-run practice has overlooked the capacity of non-state actors to conduct diplomacy, whether on an institutional or an individual level. Conducting diplomacy beyond state interests suggests that cosmopolitan values are embraced to address global challenges and negotiate win–win solutions for the parties involved. Redefining diplomacy through an expanded range of actors that perform it makes political dialogue and policy discussions more inclusive – and potentially more effective. Inclusive cosmopolitan diplomacy has been employed, both intentionally and on a coincidental basis, to pursue components of sustainable development globally, to eliminate social injustice, and to bridge the gap of global economic disparity.

Sustainable development is also crucial for achieving international security. Using Buzan et al.'s (1998) security framework for analysis, which identifies five sectors of international security, Chapter 3 explained the ways in which tourism affects each security sector and identified practices through which the international industry has been a major contributor to unsustainable models of development. This has contributed to increased levels of economic and environmental insecurity, both regionally and internationally. The discussion on tourism and international security has also revealed tourism's significant and constructive input in cases of military, political, and societal insecurity, affirming tourism stakeholders as relevant non-state actors in international political discourse.

The discussion on achieving international security and stability was followed by an examination of how tourism contributes to peace, not only by preventing insecurity and fears of violence, but also by encouraging representation and empowerment, organizational inclusivity, social justice, and resilience; factors that make peace more sustainable. The lens of critical cosmopolitanism was employed to answer the question of which forms of tourist activity can make a direct contribution to peaceful coexistence, highlighting the niche forms of peace tourism and peacebuilding tourism. Chapter 4 also stressed that peace is not pursued solely through avenues of conflict resolution mechanisms, but can also be supported through tourist-performed diplomacy, tourism that supports international development, and tourism that overturns patterns of international insecurity. Diplomacy, development, security, and peace are interlinked both as processes and as end goals. As this book underlines, the diversity of political actors active in contemporary international relations has employed tourist activities to pursue these goals collectively. Environmental activism and the objective of environmental conservation has been a common theme across these areas of international relations, and was identified as a pillar for sustainable development, as a catalyst in conflict resolution, as an objective in cosmopolitan diplomacy, and as a key concern in international security.

THE TOURIST AS AN EMERGING ACTOR IN INTERNATIONAL RELATIONS

Individual citizens have admittedly expanded their ability to engage in international affairs beyond their capacity as representatives of their affiliated states. The increasingly globalized international arena has exposed individuals from across the globe to information and data in an unprecedented manner, enabling them to not only be informed of current affairs, but also contribute to discussions, criticism, and reflections of how politics is conducted on a day-to-day basis. Access to the internet and social media, which continues to grow on an international basis, provides a platform for the political ideologies of individuals to be expressed and accessed by distant audiences, and at the same time, the ability to travel enables individuals to engage in politically informed host-visitor interactions, establish momentum for political causes, and join global movements for transnational political action. Individuals have the knowledge and means not only to deviate from the political activity their affiliated state is conducting, but also to actively embrace international relations as separate actors, joined by like-minded individuals on a transnational level, and conduct political activism – either intentionally or coincidentally – within the framework of cosmopolitan politics.

Influential tourists, like travel vloggers Lovigin and Pashkouski discussed in this book's introductory chapter, have used their tourist capacity to reach audiences from across the globe with political messages and distinguish themselves from the state entities they are citizens of. The two vloggers spoke about the currently ongoing Russian war in Ukraine and criticized EU travel sanctions that target Russian citizens instead of the state. They make the case that the tourist as a political actor has potential for significant contributions to the international political stage and their activity should be considered as separate to the activity of their affiliated state(s). The statements of the two travel vloggers, which have been shared and reproduced transnationally through news agencies and social media, provide a critical take on state-centric international policy, reaffirming the position that state governments and individual citizens can take diverging political courses and should not be treated as unitary actors in international affairs. In August 2022, the EU's discussions of a visa ban for Russian visitors were met by scepticism from France and Germany, who favoured sanctions against Russian government elites, but not sanctions that target Russian citizens (Rettman, 2022). Instead, they wish to aim for an ally among Russian citizens that are not estranged from the West, acknowledging the political input of individuals separately from the Russian state.

Differentiating between state entities and individual citizens is expectedly a priority in expanding the field of International Relations to accommodate for the input of non-state entities and individuals as international political contributors. The introductory chapter of this book presented key theories of International Relations and examined their capacity to acknowledge, explain, and evaluate individuals as political actors, with specific reference to tourists. As identified in the introductory chapter of this book, Liberalism, Constructivism, Critical Theory, and the English School entail cosmopolitan aspects that can address the political activity conducted through contemporary tourism.

Liberalism: the Tourist as a Driver of International Development

Liberalism has been a particularly popular approach in assessing the benefits of transnational collaboration on an economic level. While tourism was heralded as an avenue for wealth to be redistributed from developed to developing nations, conventional forms of mass travel and passive tourism were unable to achieve this in previous decades. Today, cosmopolitan forms of tourism are more informed and have more opportunities to engage in tourist consumption that is sustainable, and community based. By encapsulating forms of cosmopolitanism that directly inform the tourist typology spectrum and make it relevant to international relations, liberal and neoliberal theories link tourist activity to notions of democratization, free trade, global interconnectedness, and the information revolution. These aspects of the neoliberal and globalized world order allow tourism to have a substantial impact on destinations and their communities.

Nevertheless, global interconnectedness and the uninterrupted right to travel cannot alone establish win–win scenarios of mutual benefits to host and visitor audiences. The factor of cultural literacy as a measurable indicator is incorporated into the tourist typology spectrum offered in this book to specify the conditions under which culturally literate individuals can apply cosmopolitan values and empower host communities during their travels.

As the volume of international tourist activity in terms of the wealth it generates continues to grow, the dissemination of this wealth and tourism's ability to empower local communities can significantly shift local and international development dynamics. An analogous rationale informs pillars of development beyond economic wealth, with the voluminous international tourist industry being a catalyst in the use of natural resources and in human engagement with ecosystems. Chapter 1 identifies niche and emergent forms of tourism that abide by principles of equity and empowerment, and their growth in the future could have a significant impact on tourist consumption patterns internationally. Key forms of tourism to reflect on include community-based tourism, inclusive tourism, and voluntourism.

The Tourist as a Determinant of International Security: an English School Approach

Buzan and Wæver are prominent figures in advancing the English School theory and employing it to inform key approaches to international security. One such approach is the Regional Security Complex Theory, which outlines regional security dynamics in the international society of states. An additional approach to security is the sectoral framework for security analysis developed by Buzan, Wæver, and De Wilde, which offers the segmentation of security issues into the five sectors of military, political, societal, economic, and environmental security. Looking at the international political stage as a unitary field where matters of security are determined across state boundaries highlights the interconnectedness of international political agents, and thus leaves room for the impact of non-state actors to be considered.

Tourism can be identified as a determinant of international security across the five sectors of security set forth by Buzan et al. This is not surprising since tourism is a voluminous and increasingly frequent international activity that undoubtedly has the capacity to shape international patterns of mobility, consumption, and cross-cultural exchange. The example of Airbnb's intervention as a venue for humanitarian assistance in the Russia–Ukraine war in 2022 indicates that hospitality and tourism platforms can determine mobility beyond the leisure tourist and become stakeholders in refugee resettlement. At the same time, tourist consumption patterns are a significant determinant of how foreign revenue is disseminated in a host population, as well as how local resources are being consumed. Current forms of tourist consumption that follow passive, all-inclusive, and mass tourism formats are prone to reinforcing economic inequalities at the destination visited and cause large strains on environmental resources being consumed. Conscious and ethical forms of tourism have the capacity to reverse this trend and strengthen perceptions of economic and environmental security internationally.

Constructivism: the Tourist as a Contributor to Sustainable Peace

In its essence, Constructivism explains the transformational capacity of societies to escape perceptions of animosity and conflict and reconstruct social norms that embrace meaningful contact and collaboration between former rivals. Peace is directly formulated by the reconciliatory process of rebuilding social norms inclusively in societies recovering from conflict. At the same time, peace is also safeguarded when resilient societies prevent inclusive norms from being replaced by exclusive and antagonistic practices. To pursue peace is therefore a task that is inherently constructivist.

Constructivism has been defined by Wendt's text on *Anarchy is What States Make of It*, implying that the international political stage is determined by the actors engaged in international political discourse. As international tourism incorporates a significant volume of the world's mobility and transnational movement, it becomes a tool for exchanging cultural practices, informing the social norms of host destinations, and transforming the norms of individual tourists. One can therefore argue that the world stage is what tourists make of it: they can utilize their mobility to transform social norms towards inclusive, sustainable, and ethical practices, and as such become active agents in transnational sociopolitical change. Tourist activity will occur more and more frequently in the decades to come, and this momentum has the potential to craft a more resilient, cosmopolitan, and culturally literate world.

Distinguishing between active cosmopolitan forms of tourism and unethical and unsustainable ones is again a process of social construction. Tourism is a multiphasic experience that commences at the decision-making stage before travelling to a destination and engaging in visitor experiences there. A tourist experience can be broken down into five stages: the conception stage, the transportation stage, the destination stage, the return stage, and the recollection stage. Social norms informing each of these stages can be revisited and reconceptualized through cosmopolitan values in a way that will prevent harmful forms of tourism from being performed. A pro-peace global civil society with transnational momentum can inform all five stages of a tourism experience and generate interest in peace-oriented forms of travel.

Socially constructed norms, particularly of international appeal, can inform the tourist's individual tastes and preferences. Employing Neulinger's notion of leisure as a state of mind, the tourist can experience leisure by engaging in activities that yield personal eudaimonia and satisfaction, and not necessarily in activities that are conventionally labeled as leisure. Neulinger (1984) states that leisure can be achieved as a state of mind if the individual engages in an activity with perceived freedom of choice and motivated entirely by internal factors. Accordingly, when the tourist finds happiness and satisfaction through forms of critical cosmopolitan travel, it is more likely for these forms of conducive tourism to expand and become a popular transnational norm.

Critical Theory: the Tourist as a Non-state Political Actor

The principal contribution of Critical Theory in addressing the relationship between tourism and international relations is the ability of this theoretical framework to challenge assumptions in the field that take existing power dynamics and political actor hierarchies as externally granted. To this end, out of the entire theoretical spectrum in IR, Critical Theory is the theory most capable of introducing new actors in international affairs, questioning existing structures and political patterns, and providing new angles to define international politics. The Critical Theory angle explains that the tourist can be acknowledged as a non-state political actor, not necessarily as a new actor, but more so as a stakeholder in international affairs that had thus far been overlooked.

Critical Theory's contributions to the study of international relations focus on revealing inequalities, shifting unjust power dynamics, and identifying opportunities for equity, agency, and empowerment. This also includes, through some of the theory's streams, a focus on language and its ability to reinforce stereotypes and inequalities. This theoretical underpinning enables Tourism studies to revisit the wider spectrum of international tourist activity and more effectively identify tourist practices that are ethical, emancipatory, and supportive of social equity, and distinguish them from tourist activity that is unethical and harmful to host communities. Fostering and promoting the former, which is encapsulated under the critical cosmopolitan tourist typology, establishes a clear reference point for treating the tourist as a non-state political actor.

Tourism as a Form of International Relations: the Neorealist Perspective

While Realism follows a positivist and state-centric theoretical approach that is less suitable to discuss atypical non-state actors, tourist-performed political activity has direct implications for state actors that can be most effectively revealed through state-centric theoretical angles. Neorealism suggests that international relations are driven by state actors and the interests they pursue. Their international political activity is shaped by the structural realities and dynamics provided by the international political stage within a given time-frame. In the post-pandemic era, the interconnectedness of state actors calls for coordinated state action towards key policy priorities, including economic progress, environmental action, and political stability.

The international migration crisis, experienced most severely within the five-year period before the COVID-19 pandemic (2015–2020), was characterized by unprecedented waves of migrants coming into Western states, including the United States, Canada, and member states of the European Union. The migration crisis was soon securitized across Western audiences, who saw the voluminous flows of migrants as an imminent threat to economic and societal security. In the United States and the United Kingdom, rhetoric against the threat of migrants cultivated into a populist insurgence that brought anti-migration leaders such as Donald Trump and Boris Johnson into power.

While an initial response to the migration crisis was strict controls and restrictions on cross-border movement, the West requires a long-term strategy to address future migration patterns including not only conflict-related migration, but also economic and environmental migration. There is a shared incentive in addressing destinations at risk and contributing to their future stability and resilience.

Forms of public and citizen diplomacy with the capacity to empower and strengthen communities at risk could therefore directly serve Western state interests through their tourist activity and the exchange of best practices with these host communities. Moving beyond basic forms of voluntourism, top-down third-party interventions, and dynamics of the white saviour complex, forms of critical cosmopolitan tourism can establish structures of community empowerment, reciprocal communication, and local agency. States, as well as supranational entities such as the UN, can create channels for tourism to destinations at risk, and provide incentives for global civil society movements and individual experts to engage with communities lacking resilience and sustainable practices. Employing tourism as a mechanism for establishing sustainable peace and community resilience and bringing together hosts and visitors through organic structures of meaningful exchange can generate incentives for local audiences to achieve stability and growth at home and avoid involuntary migration due to imminent existential threats.

The EU offers the example of Erasmus exchange programmes to enhance European citizenship and culture through educational and cultural exchanges. An analogous exchange programme beyond Western territories and across civilizations can serve as a starting point to meaningful citizen-led dialogue that can yield community empowerment and support in times of risk. In these scenarios, the critical cosmopolitan tourist is not motivated by a desire for recreation, but by their willingness to contribute to international stability through politically informed and culturally literate travel. Admittedly, the role of tourism in the international migration crisis is predominantly preventative. The tourist does not have significant leverage to reactively respond to international migrant flows with border restrictions or financial reallocation in a manner analogous to states. Nevertheless, tourism holds significant capacity in establishing sustainable dynamics and increased international security that can prevent similar and more severe migration crises in the future.

TOURISM AS A FORM OF INTERNATIONAL RELATIONS: THEORETICAL LIMITATIONS AND OPPORTUNITIES

Undoubtedly, the tourist as a non-state political actor has a role to play in contemporary international relations. Existing theoretical frameworks are able, to a certain extent, to embrace this observation and articulate its input. At the same time, however, this analysis reveals that there are certain theoretical limitations in doing so and identifies the need to look beyond the conventional IR theories that were developed with state actors in mind.

When existing IR theories face restrictions in illustrating the bigger picture of how international political activity is conducted – through the multitude of actors performing it both intentionally and coincidentally – a course of action to consider is, while expanding the scope of contemporary international relations, to also expand the theoretical frameworks through which these are studied. To this end, one of the future directions this volume of work suggests is the need for post-disciplinary, cosmopolitan avenues for research. This will enable the IR field to move beyond current theoretical frameworks and towards tourism-informed theories of International Relations that will more effectively acknowledge the agency of individuals on the international political stage, particularly those individuals that engage with the voluntary mobility that tourism offers.

Reviewing insights of contemporary practice that indicate tourism's socio-political contributions on the international stage has also revealed a lack of tourist activity in certain areas of International Relations. An evident example comes through cosmopolitan diplomacy and the Blue Peace Index, which identified resource mismanagement and lack of cooperation across the state actors involved in the use of water from specific river basins that span across national borders. While there is potential for citizen-led cosmopolitan diplomacy through tourism to support state actors in shared resource management – or other challenges that reach a deadlock due to persistent state-oriented interests – more efforts to realize this potential should be employed to grant critical cosmopolitan tourists with the right platforms for political engagement.

This observed scarcity of tourist-performed cosmopolitan diplomacy signals not a lack of prospects for its effectiveness and future impact, but a need for global civil society and the international community to establish more avenues through which the input and communication of individual tourists can be recorded and embedded into a broader structured diplomatic discourse. Beyond the example of the Blue Peace Index, individual exchanges between host and visitor audiences across the world can be recorded on the topics of sustainability, equality, inclusivity, economic welfare, and environmental conservation. While the input of citizens has traditionally been recorded indirectly through governmental representatives or through grassroots initiatives and civil society institutions, the possibility to provide platforms for structured and theme-specific exchanges between hosts and visitors across destinations can significantly broaden the democratic capacities of political representation on a transnational, cosmopolitan level.

FUTURE DIRECTIONS

Towards a More Inclusive Examination of International Relations

A key challenge for the IR field has been its focus on a certain type of international political actors, sovereign states, as well as the fact that for much of the field's evolution, IR studies assumed a Western-oriented angle. These assumptions informing the field's ontology and epistemology are now acknowledged as patterns of exclusivity in the field's examination of international affairs, which eventually led to criticisms of the IR field's inability to effectively predict global phenomena.

Today, academia has proceeded to engage non-Western and post-Western perspectives in the examination of international affairs, while non-state actors and their political activity have received closer attention. These are steps that have managed to make the field of International Relations more inclusive in terms of ontological perspectives and with regards to the international political actors examined. A more inclusive IR field has the capacity to achieve more comprehensive and well-rounded accounts of international political phenomena, and thus to increase its ability to identify, understand, evaluate, and predict dynamics in global affairs.

The bridge between Tourism and IR comes in line with the current momentum to broaden the scope of International Relations. Discussing tourism as a form of international relations does not only allow for an additional actor to be considered. It additionally informs IR dynamics through the world's most voluminous international activity; if more than one billion people engage in tourism annually, then more than one billion global actors perform international activities with political consequences, yielding either intentional political impact or coincidental – and often overlooked – outputs. Understanding individuals as political agents when engaging in voluntary, non-migrational, short-term travel, opens an entire spectrum of political activity that has not been considered so far.

As the chapters of this book have revealed, tourism has the capacity to endorse global inequalities, to reinforce negative stereotypes, to spread cross-cultural prejudice, and to exacerbate international environmental and economic insecurity. It can also act as an indicator of safety and stability in a destination, generate economic growth for isolated communities, drive environmental conservation, and push against social injustice. Undoubtedly, tourist activity affects global phenomena and international socio-political dynamics. To this end, any attempt to broaden the scholarly scope of International Relations should first consider tourism's international activity that is influential to international political affairs but has not thus far been labelled as "political activity".

To incorporate tourism into the field of International Relations, this book employed critical cosmopolitanism as an appropriate theoretical angle that revealed the magnitude to which tourism can shape international political agency, both for tourists and for host communities. On the one hand, tourists as consumers and diplomats can choose a self-oriented decision-making approach to their travel itinerary, and neglect whether their consumption, attitude, and exchange with host populations could lead to the reinforcement of inequalities, to socioeconomic misfortunes for locals, and to environmental degradation. On the other hand, tourists equipped with acute cultural literacy and cosmopolitan values that prioritize the interconnectedness and interde-pendency of hosts and visitors in tourism are likely to formulate their tourist activities in ways that strengthen host populations, favour sustainability, and create platforms for coordinated transnational socio-political action.

Indisputably, incorporating tourism into the realm of international political activity can reveal significant observations about how individuals shape global dynamics. Identifying the impact of individual tourist behaviour on interna-tional affairs, phenomena, and perceptions can directly inform International Relations, identify formerly neglected global patterns, and increase the field's capacity to predict the course of international politics. Examining the rela-tionship between tourism and international relations from the perspective of critical cosmopolitanism as employed in this book suggests that informing the IR field through trends in international tourist activity enables an improved and more comprehensive understanding of international political interaction.

Source: Author.

Figure 5.1   *Tourism's contribution to international relations*

Figure 5.1 illustrates how cosmopolitan forms of tourism lead to more inclusive international relations.

Critical cosmopolitan tourism, as presented in Figure 5.1, refers to the forms of tourism that uphold cosmopolitan values and are attentive to dynamics of equity and social justice when traveling and interacting with host populations. Defining critical cosmopolitan tourism in this context is different from Urry's (1996) definition of the cosmopolitan tourist as the traveller with the right to access and consume all environments. Critical forms of cosmopolitan tourism are presented in more detail in Chapter 1, which examines the impact of tourism informed by cosmopolitan values with reference to the Sustainable Development Goals. Critical cosmopolitan tourists are found at the allocentric end of the Tourist Typology Spectrum (Figure 1.2). They affiliate with the allocentric, drifter, and venturer tourist typologies, show high likelihood to embrace cosmopolitan values in their tourist activity, and show increased levels of cross-cultural literacy. With reference to diplomacy, the critical cosmopolitan tourist is likely to perform intentional cosmopolitan diplomacy during their travels. With regards to international security, this audience of tourists are the most likely to customize their travel experiences and tourism consumption activities in ways that prevent environmental, economic, or other forms of insecurity, and empower host communities. The critical cosmopolitan tourist is also likely to employ personal and professional skills and, through their tourist capacity, to contribute to a destination's efforts for peace, stability, and resilience.

Towards a Quantitative Examination of Tourism's Contribution to International Relations

Throughout this book's last chapters, peace has been heralded as a comprehensive end goal for societies globally. The notion of peace incorporates the diverse facets of societal progress, reflects transparent and inclusive governance, embraces sustainable development, and is characterized by security and resilience. Considerable academic and practitioner efforts have been made to increase our ability to measure peace. Peace as a more tangible and measurable end goal allows us to identify whether social progress, stability, and cohesion is achieved to a satisfactory level and, if not, which are the factors that put this objective at risk. Measuring peace is a vital tool not only for de-escalating a conflict and establishing the conditions for reconciliation, but it is also critical for societies whose levels of inclusivity, welfare, and social justice are low and thus the likelihood for a future conflict to escalate is high. The Blue Peace Index offers a clear assessment of transnational water management across states sharing a river basin, featuring both best practices as well as examples of severe mismanagement. The Global Peace Index delves into the relationship between negative and positive peace and features the positive peace deficit as an indicator of a country's discrepancy between the lack of violence and the truly peaceful coexistence among its members. The SCORE index calculates a country's level of success in achieving social cohesion, particularly across rival communities, and hence evaluates their progress in processes of reconciliation. The variety of quantified perspectives these indices offer on peace allow for a universal understanding of peace and make obstacles and threats to peace identifiable and preventable.

Notions such as peace, sustainable development, and the socio-political impacts of tourism have thus far been flagged as vague and difficult to illustrate in numbers. Achieving the quantification of the tourism and peace relationship can expand the discussion of tourism's contribution to peace beyond its qualitative assessment, with tools that are already available for the study of peace. A quantitative assessment of the peace-through-tourism relationship can then expand to incorporate quantitative assessments of tourist's contribution to sustainable development – through the tangible indicators and metrics that the SDG framework has established – and advance these metrics to introduce associations between tourism and diplomacy, as well as tourism and international security. Employing these perspectives as measurable components of the tourist's contributions as a non-state political actor can develop a quantitative analytical tool of a new and more inclusive field of international relations altogether.

CONCLUSION

Introducing the tourist as a non-state political actor immediately expands the scope of international relations and provides a broader framework of international political activity to be considered. The critical cosmopolitan tourist makes international relations not only more inclusive by broadening its scope of political activity, but also more comprehensive when explaining international phenomena and dynamics. Engaging more actors on the international political stage achieves increased diversity and inclusivity both for conducting and for examining international affairs. Involving actors that have been thus far overlooked, particularly individuals, takes international relations beyond exclusive and elitist channels of political communication, achieving empowerment and emancipation for the unconventional audiences included.

There are practical dimensions to expanding the scope of international relations, and policy recommendations to be made. Engaging unconventional actors in international political discourse implies creating appropriate platforms through which the magnitude of political input provided can be structured and disseminated across policy-making forums. Engaging individuals in formal political communication beyond grassroot channels, encouraging tourists to engage in emancipatory and culturally literate visitor–host exchanges, and establishing more platforms for intentional cosmopolitan diplomacy can enhance the opportunities through which tourists can contribute to sustainable development, peace, stability, and community resilience. Examining, supporting, and generating critical cosmopolitan tourism can have a considerable impact on how international relations are conducted in the future, and to what extent inclusive and participatory international politics can shape human interaction in the decades to come.

References

Abbate, C. S. & Di Nuovo, S. (2013). Motivation and personality traits for choosing religious tourism: A research on the case of Medjugorje. *Current Issues in Tourism*, 16(5), 501–506.

Acharya, A. (2014). Global international relations (IR) and regional worlds: A new agenda for international studies. *International Studies Quarterly*, 58(4), 647–659.

Adam, H. & Moodley, K. (2005). *Seeking Mandela: Peacemaking between Israelis and Palestinians*. Temple University Press.

Airbnb (2022). Host people fleeing Ukraine. Airbnb.org https://www.airbnb.org/help -ukraine. Accessed on 16 March 2022.

Akhtar, M. (2022). Is booking Airbnbs really the best way to help Ukrainians? *Vox*. https://www.vox.com/22973133/ukraine-russia-airbnb-booking-donate-effective-alt ruism. Accessed on 16 March 2022.

Ali, S. & Vladich, H. (2016). Environmental diplomacy. In C. Constantinou, P. Kerr & P. Sharp (eds), *The SAGE Handbook of Diplomacy*, SAGE Publishing, pp. 601–616.

Alkire, S. (2010). Human development: Definitions, critiques, and related concepts. *OPHI Working Paper* No. 36, SSRN.

Allport, G. (1954). *The Nature of Prejudice*. Cambridge: Addison-Wesley Publishing Company, Inc.

Amin, A. (1994). Post-Fordism: Models, fantasies and phantoms of transition. In A. Amin (ed.), *Post-Fordism: A Reader*, Oxford: Blackwell, pp. 1–40.

Anastasopoulos, P. G. (1992). Tourism and attitude change: Greek tourists visiting Turkey. *Annals of Tourism Research*, 19(4), 629–642.

Anderson, R. (2004). A definition of peace. *Peace and Conflict: Journal of Peace Psychology*, 10(2), 101.

Ang, I., Isar, Y. R., & Mar, P. (2015). Cultural diplomacy: Beyond the national interest? *International Journal of Cultural Policy*, 21(4), 365–381.

Anton, A. (2022). Conceptual pathways to civil society diplomacy. In S. P. Sebastião & S. de Carvalho Spínola (eds), *Diplomacy, Organisations and Citizens*, Cham: Springer, pp. 81–98.

Antoniou, K. (2021). Post-pandemic travel: The trends we'll see when the world opens up again. *The Conversation*, April 8.

Antoniou, K. (2021). The role of visiting professionals in peacebuilding. In J. T. da Silva, Z. Breda & F. Carbone (eds), *Role and Impact of Tourism in Peacebuilding and Conflict Transformation*, IGI Global, pp. 320–341.

Antoniou, K. (2022). Peer-to-peer accommodation as a peacebuilding tool: Community resilience and group membership. In A. Farmaki, D. Ioannides & S. Kladou (eds), *Peer-to-peer Accommodation and Community Resilience: Implications for Sustainable Development*, CAB International, p. 111.

Antoniou, K. (2022a). Peace tourism. In D. Buhalis (ed.), *Encyclopedia of Tourism Management and Marketing* (Vol. 3), Cheltenham, UK and Northampton, MA, USA: Edward Elgar Publishing, pp. 448–451.

Antoniou, K. (2022b). Peacebuilding Tourism. In D. Buhalis (ed.), *Encyclopedia of Tourism Management and Marketing* (Vol. 3), Cheltenham, UK and Northampton, MA, USA: Edward Elgar Publishing, pp. 456–459.

Ap, J. & Var, T. (1990). Does tourism promote world peace? *Tourism Management*, 11(3), 267–273.

Apostolides, A., Apostolides, C., & Güryay, E. (2012). From conflict to economic interdependence in Cyprus. *Peace Review*, 24(4), 430–437.

Araña, J. E. & León, C. J. (2008). The impact of terrorism on tourism demand. *Annals of Tourism Research*, 35(2), 299–315.

Aulet, S. & Tarrés, E. (2021). Tourism and peacebuilding from a holistic approach: The case of trails for peace. In J. T. da Silva, Z. Breda & F. Carbone (eds), *Role and Impact of Tourism in Peacebuilding and Conflict Transformation*, IGI Global, pp. 46–65.

Aydınlı, E. & Biltekin, G. (2018). Introduction: Widening the world of IR. In E. Aydınlı & G. Biltekin (eds), *Widening the World of International Relations*, Routledge, pp. 1–12.

Baranowski, S., Covert, L. P., Gordon, B. M., Jobs, R. I., Noack, C., Rosenbaum, A. T., & Scott, B. C. (2019). Discussion: Tourism and diplomacy. *Journal of Tourism History*, 11(1), 63–90.

Bar-Tal, D. & Bennink, G.H. (2004). The nature of reconciliation as an outcome and as a process. In Y. Bar-Siman-Tov (ed.), *From Conflict Resolution to Reconciliation*, Oxford: Oxford University Press, pp. 11–27.

Beck, U. (2007). Cosmopolitanism: A critical theory for the twenty-first century. In G. Ritzer (ed.), *The Blackwell Companion to Globalization*, Blackwell Publishing, pp. 162–176.

Bellamy, A. J. (2009). *Responsibility to Protect*. Polity.

Benjamin, S., Dillette, A., & Alderman, D. H. (2020). "We can't return to normal": Committing to tourism equity in the post-pandemic age. *Tourism Geographies*, 22(3), 476–483.

Bercovitch, J. (1996). Thinking about mediation. In J. Bercovitch (ed.), *Resolving International Conflicts: the Theory and Practice of Mediation*, London: Lynne Rienner Publishers Inc, pp. 1–10.

Bianchi, R. V. & Stephenson, M. L. (2013). Deciphering tourism and citizenship in a globalized world. *Tourism Management*, 39, 10–20.

Biddle, P. (2014). Why I stopped being a voluntourist. *Tourism Concern*, 13 September 2014.

Biran, A. & Poria, Y. (2012). Reconceptualizing dark tourism. In R. Sharpley and P. Stone (eds), *Contemporary Tourist Experience: Concepts and Consequences*, Oxon: Routledge, pp. 59–70.

Biran, A., Poria, Y., & Oren, G. (2011). Sought experiences at (dark) heritage sites. *Annals of Tourism Research*, 38(3), 820–841.

Bishara, M. (2001). *Palestine/Israel: Peace or Apartheid: Prospects for Resolving the Conflict*. Canada: Fernwood Publishing.

Blanchard, L. A. & Higgins-Desbiolles, F. (2013). *Peace through Tourism: Promoting Human Security Through International Citizenship*, Oxon: Routledge.

Blaser, M. (2016). Is another cosmopolitics possible? *Cultural Anthropology*, 31(4), 545–570.

Boehmer, E. (2008). *Nelson Mandela: A Very Short Introduction*, Vol. 188, Oxford: Oxford University Press.

Bolaji-Adio, A. (2015). The challenge of measuring SDG 16. *European Centre for Development Policy Management*, 175.

Bozkurt, U. (2012). Westernization. *The Wiley-Blackwell Encyclopedia of Globalization*.

Bradley Phillips, A. (2007). Constructivism. In M. Griffiths (ed.), *International Relations Theory for the Twenty-first Century: An Introduction*, New York: Routledge, pp. 60–74.

Brown, P. & Lauder, H. (1996). Education, globalization, and economic development. *Journal of Education Policy*, 11(1), 1–25.

Bull, H. (1977). *The Anarchical Society: A Study of Order in World Politics*, New York: Columbia University Press.

Bull, H. (1984). *Justice in International Relations*. The Hagey Lectures, Waterloo, Ont.

Bulmer, S. & Paterson, W. E. (2013). Germany as the EU's reluctant hegemon? Of economic strength and political constraints. *Journal of European Public Policy*, 20(10), 1387–1405.

Bunakov, O. A., Eidelman, B. M., Fakhrutdinova, L. R., & Gabdrakhmanov, N. K. (2018). Tourism as a method of "soft power" in modern diplomacy on the example of the Russian Federation. *Helix*, 8(1), 2174–2177.

Burchill, S. (2009). Liberalism. In S. Burchill, A. Linklater, R. Devetak, J. Donelly, T. Nardin, M. Patterson, C. Reus-Smit & J. True (eds), *Theories of International Relations*, 4th ed., London: Palgrave Macmillan, pp. 57–85.

Burchill, S., Linklater, A., Devetak, R., Donelly, J., Nardin, T., Patterson, M., Reus-Smit, C. & True, J. (2009). *Theories of International Relations*, 4th ed., London: Palgrave Macmillan.

Butler, M. (2012). *Selling a "Just" War: Framing, Legitimacy, and US Military Intervention*, London: Palgrave Macmillan.

Butler, M. (Ed.). (2020). *Securitization, Revisited*, Abingdon: Routledge.

Buzan, B. (2004). *From International Society to World Society? English School Theory and the Social Structure of Globalisation*, Cambridge University Press.

Buzan, B. G. & Wæver, O. (2003). *Regions and Powers: The Structure of International Security* (Vol. 91), Cambridge University Press.

Buzan, B., Wæver, O., & De Wilde, J. (1998). *Security: A new framework for analysis*, Lynne Rienner Publishers.

Cameron, F. (2002). *US Foreign Policy after the Cold War: Global Hegemon or Reluctant Sheriff?* Oxon: Routledge.

Carbone, F. (2020). Tourism destination management post COVID-19 pandemic: A new humanism for a human-centered tourism (tourism 5.0). *Turismo Mundial, Crise Sanitária e Futuro*, 43.

Carbone, F. & Oosterbeek, L. (2021). Peace: A Roadmap for Heritage and Tourism. In J. T. da Silva, Z. Breda & F. Carbone (eds), *Role and Impact of Tourism in Peacebuilding and Conflict Transformation*, IGI Global, pp. 1–15.

Cheah, P. (2006). Cosmopolitanism. *Theory, Culture & Society*, 23(2–3), 486–496.

Cohen, E. (1972). Toward a sociology of international tourism. *Social Research*, 164–182.

Cohen, E. (2008). The changing faces of contemporary tourism. *Society*, 45(4), 330–333.

Cohen, E. (2011). Educational dark tourism at an in populo site: The Holocaust Museum in Jerusalem. *Annals of Tourism Research*, 38(1), 193–209.

Cohen, R. (2013). Diplomacy through the ages. In P. Kerr & G. Wiseman (eds), *Diplomacy in a Globalizing World: Theories and Practices*, Oxford University Press.

Colin T. J., Clemmitt, M., Cooper, M. H., Glazer, S., Jost, K., Katel, P., Marshall, P., Masci, D., & Standen, A. (2007). *Global Issues: Selections from the CQ Researcher*, Washington DC: CQ Press.

Cooley, A. & Nexon, D. H. (2020). How hegemony ends. *Foreign Affairs*, 99, 143.

Couchsurfing (2022). https://about.couchsurfing.com/about/about-us/. Accessed on 20 June 2022.

D'Amore, L. J. (1988). Tourism: A vital force for peace. *Annals of Tourism Research*, 15, 269–283.

Daly, H. E. (2006). Sustainable development – definitions, principles, policies. In M. Keiner (ed.), *The Future of Sustainability*, Dordrecht: Springer, pp. 39–53.

Dann, G. M. (1977). Anomie, ego-enhancement and tourism. *Annals of Tourism Research*, 4(4), 184–194.

Delanty, G. & Harris, N. (2018). The idea of critical cosmopolitanism. In *Routledge International Handbook of Cosmopolitanism Studies*, Routledge, pp. 91–100.

Devetak, R. (2009). Critical theory. In S. Burchill, A. Linklater, R. Devetak, J. Donelly, T. Nardin, M. Patterson, C. Reus-Smit & J. True (eds), *Theories of International Relations*, 4th ed., London: Palgrave Macmillan, pp. 159–182.

Dickinson, J. E. (2022). Slow travel. In D. Buhalis (ed.), *Encyclopedia of Tourism Management and Marketing* (Vol. 4), Cheltenham, UK and Northampton, MA, USA: Edward Elgar Publishing, pp. 107–109.

Donnelly, J. (2009). Realism. In S. Burchill, A. Linklater, R. Devetak, J. Donelly, T. Nardin, M. Patterson, C. Reus-Smit & J. True (eds), *Theories of International Relations*, 4th ed., London: Palgrave Macmillan, pp. 31–56.

Ducharme, J. (2020). World Health Organization declares COVID-19 a "Pandemic": Here's what that means. *TIME*, March 11, 2020. https://time.com/5791661/who -coronavirus-pandemic-declaration/. Accessed on 17 December 2021.

Dujmović, M. & Vitasović, A. (2015). Postmodern society and tourism. *Journal of Tourism and Hospitality Management*, 3(9–10), 192–203.

Dwyer, L. (2015). Globalization of tourism: Drivers and outcomes. *Tourism Recreation Research*, 40(3), 326–339.

Easterly, W. R. (2002). *The Elusive Quest for Growth: Economists' Adventures and Misadventures in the Tropics*, MIT Press.

Economist Impact (2022). Blue Peace Index. *The Economist.* Blue Peace Index | Economist Intelligence Unit. Accessed on 25 August 2022.

Engelmann, J., Al-Saidi, M., & Hamhaber, J. (2019). Concretizing green growth and sustainable business models in the water sector of Jordan. *Resources*, 8(2), 92.

European Commission (2020). 21 December 2020 – European Commission authorizes first safe and effective vaccine against COVID-19, *September to December 2020 Highlights*. https://ec.europa.eu/info/live-work-travel-eu/coronavirus-response/high lights/september-december-2020_en. Accessed on 17 December 2021.

Everett, S. (2008). Beyond the visual gaze? The pursuit of an embodied experience through food tourism. *Tourist Studies*, 8(3), 337–358.

Farmaki, A. (2017). The tourism and peace nexus. *Tourism Management*, 59, 528–540.

Farmaki, A. (2022). Peace and tourism. In D. Buhalis (ed.), *Encyclopedia of Tourism Management and Marketing* (Vol. 3), Cheltenham, UK and Northampton, MA, USA: Edward Elgar Publishing, pp. 451–453.

Farmaki, A. & Stergiou, D. (2021). Peace and tourism: Bridging the gap through justice. *Peace & Change*, 46(3), 286–309.

Feigenbaum, E. A. (2008). China's challenge to Pax Americana. In A. T. J. Lennon & A. Kozlowski (eds), *Global Powers in the 21st Century: Strategies and Relations*, MIT Press.

Finkelstein, L. S. (1995). What is global governance. *Global Governance*, 1, 367.

Fisher, R. J. (1993). The potential for peacebuilding: Forging a bridge from peacekeeping to peacemaking. *Peace and Change*, 18(3), 247–266.

Fisher, R. J. (1997). *Interactive Conflict Resolution*, New York: Syracuse University Press.

Flower, E. K., Burns, G. L., Jones, D. N., & McBroom, J. (2021). Does the experience make a difference? Comparing tourist attitudes pre-and post-visit towards the elephant tourism industry. *Annals of Tourism Research Empirical Insights*, 2(2), 100025.

Foley, M. & Lennon, J. J. (1996). JFK and dark tourism: A fascination with assassination. *International Journal of Heritage Studies*, 2(4), 198–211.

Fortna, V. P. (2008). *Does Peacekeeping Work?* Princeton University Press.

Friedman, T. L. (2005). *The World is Flat: A Brief History of the Twenty-first Century*, Macmillan.

Fukuyama, F. (1989). The end of history? *The National Interest*, 16, 3–18.

Fullerton, J. A. & Kendrick, A. (2013). Strategic uses of mediated public diplomacy: International reaction to US tourism advertising. *American Behavioral Scientist*, 57(9), 1332–1349.

Galtung, J. (1969). Violence, peace, and peace research. *Journal of Peace Research*, 6(3), 167–191.

Gilboa, E. (2008). Searching for a theory of public diplomacy. *Annals of the American Academy of Political and Social Science*, 616(1), 55–77.

Global Issues 2007: Selections from the CQ Researcher. CQ Press.

Global Issues 2022: Selections from the CQ Researcher. CQ Press.

Goodwin, H. (2022). Responsible tourism. In D. Buhalis (ed.), *Encyclopedia of Tourism Management and Marketing* (Vol. 3), Cheltenham, UK and Northampton, MA, USA: Edward Elgar Publishing, pp. 711–714.

Gössling, S., Peeters, P., Hall, C. M., Ceron, J. P., Dubois, G., & Scott, D. (2012). Tourism and water use: Supply, demand, and security. An international review. *Tourism Management*, 33(1), 1–15.

Gössling, S., Scott, D., & Hall, C. M. (2021). Pandemics, tourism and global change: A rapid assessment of COVID-19. *Journal of Sustainable Tourism*, 29(1), 1–20.

Gould, K. (April 2019). The white savior complex: The dark side of volunteering [video]. *TED Conferences. The White Savior Complex: The Dark Side of Volunteering | Kayley Gould | TEDxLAHS*.

Gregory, B. (2016). Mapping boundaries in diplomacy's public dimension. *The Hague Journal of Diplomacy*, 11(1), 1–25.

Gross, L. (1948). The Peace of Westphalia, 1648–1948. *American Journal of International Law*, 42(1), 20–41.

Gu, Z., Gao, X., & Ryu, S. (2022). Public diplomacy as a determinant of bilateral tourism between the influencer and influencee countries: Evidence from the Asia-Pacific region. *Asia Pacific Journal of Tourism Research*, 27(3), 319–330.

Gulmez, S. B. (2018). Cosmopolitan diplomacy. In *Routledge International Handbook of Cosmopolitanism Studies*, Routledge, pp. 430–439.

Guzzini, S. (2000). A reconstruction of constructivism in international relations. *European Journal of International Relations*, 6(2), 147–182.

Haeck, P. (2022). Airbnb's pledge to house Ukrainian refugees gets a reality check. *Politico*. https://www.politico.eu/article/airbnb-pledge-target-house-ukranian-refugees-reality-check/. Accessed on 16 March 2022.

Hafner-Burton, E. M., Kahler, M., & Montgomery, A. H. (2009). Network analysis for international relations. *International Organization*, 63(3), 559–592.

Hall, C. M. (2014). Framing behavioural approaches to understanding and governing sustainable tourism consumption: beyond neoliberalism, "nudging" and "green growth"? In S. A. Cohen, J. E. S. Higham, S. Gossling & P. Peeters (eds), *Understanding and Governing Sustainable Tourism Mobility*, Routledge, pp. 296–319.

Hall, C. M., Timothy, D. J., & Duval, D. T. (2004). Security and tourism: Towards a new understanding? *Journal of Travel & Tourism Marketing*, 15(2–3), 1–18.

Hall, S. (1988). Brave new world. *Marxism Today*, October, 24–29.

Hannay, D. (2005). *Cyprus: The Search for a Solution*, London: I.B. Tauris and Co Ltd.

Heisbourg, F. (1999). American hegemony? Perceptions of the US abroad. *Survival*, 41(4), 5–19.

Heitmann, S. (2011). Authenticity in tourism. In P. Robinson, S. Heitmann & P. U. C. Dieke (eds), *Research Themes for Tourism*, CABI, pp. 45–58.

Henderson, J. C., Shufen, C., Huifen, L., & Xiang, L. L. (2010). Tourism and terrorism: A hotel industry perspective. *Journal of Tourism, Hospitality & Culinary Arts* (JTHCA), 2(1), 1–14.

Hettne, B. (2002). In search of world order. In B. Hettne & B. Oden (eds), *Global Governance in the 21st Century: Alternative Perspectives on World Order*, Stockholm: Almkvist and Wiksell International, pp. 6–25.

Hirst, P. & Zeitlin, J. (1991). Flexible specialization versus post-Fordism: Theory, evidence and policy implications. *Economy and Society*, 20(1), 5–9.

Hoff, P. D. & Ward, M. D. (2004). Modeling dependencies in international relations networks. *Political Analysis*, 12(2), 160–175.

Holzscheiter, A. (2005). Discourse as capability: Non-state actors' capital in global governance. *Millennium: Journal of International Studies*, 33(3), 723–746.

Huntington, S. P. (1993). The clash of civilizations? *Foreign Affairs*, 72(3), 22–49.

Iglesias, M. (2022). Language tourism. In D. Buhalis (ed.), *Encyclopedia of Tourism Management and Marketing* (Vol. 3), Cheltenham, UK and Northampton, MA, USA: Edward Elgar Publishing, pp. 35–37.

Ivanovic, A., Cooper, H., & Nguyen, A. M. (2018). Institutionalisation of SDG 16: More a trickle than a cascade? *Social Alternatives*, 37(1), 49–57.

Jamgade, S. (2021). Catalytic effect of tourism in peacebuilding: Sustainability and peace through tourism. In J. T. da Silva, Z. Bread & F. Carbone (eds), *Role and Impact of Tourism in Peacebuilding and Conflict Transformation*, IGI Global, pp. 29–45.

Jarraud, N. & Lordos, A. (2012). Participatory approaches to environmental conflict resolution in Cyprus. *Conflict Resolution Quarterly*, 29(3), 261–281.

Johnsen, C. G., Nelund, M., Olaison, L., & Meier Sørensen, B. (2017). Organizing for the post-growth economy. *Ephemera: Theory and Politics in Organization*, 17(1), 1–21.

Johnson, P. C. (2014). Cultural literacy, cosmopolitanism and tourism research. *Annals of Tourism Research*, 44, 255–269.

Kaldor, M. (1999). *New and Old Wars: Organized Violence in a Global Era*, California: Stanford University Press.

Kaldor, M. (2001). *New and Old Wars*, California: Stanford University Press.

Kaldor, M. (2003). The idea of global civil society. *International Affairs*, 79(3), 583–593.

Kaldor, M. (2020). Global civil society: An answer to war. In S. Seidman & J. C. Alexander (eds), *The New Social Theory Reader*, Routledge, pp. 252–259.

Kapur, G. (1997). Globalisation and culture. *Third Text*, 11(39), 21–38.

Keane, J. (2003). *Global Civil Society?* Cambridge University Press.

Kepher-Gona, J. & Atieno, L. (2022). Community-based tourism in Africa. In D. Buhalis (ed.), *Encyclopedia of Tourism Management and Marketing* (Vol. 1), Cheltenham, UK and Northampton, MA, USA: Edward Elgar Publishing, pp. 577–580.

Kerr, P. & Taylor, B. (2013). Track-Two diplomacy in East Asia. In P. Kerr & G. Wiseman (eds), *Diplomacy in a Globalizing World: Theories and Practices*, Oxford University Press, pp. 226–243.

Kerr, P. & Wiseman, G. (2013). *Diplomacy in a Globalizing World: Theories and Practices*, Oxford University Press.

Kissinger, H. (1994). *Diplomacy*, Simon and Schuster.

Kornioti, N. & Antoniou, K. (2022). Social mediation as a grassroots method fostering sustainable community collaboration. *IMPACT Journal*, 2.

Korstanje, M. E. & Clayton, A. (2012). Tourism and terrorism: Conflicts and commonalities. *Worldwide Hospitality and Tourism Themes*, 4(1), 8–25.

Krasner, S. D. (1996). Compromising Westphalia. *International Security*, 20(3), 115–151.

Krasner, S. D. (1999). *Sovereignty: Organized Hypocrisy*, Princeton University Press.

Krauthammer, C. (1989). Universal dominion: Toward a unipolar world. *The National Interest*, 18, 46–49.

Kucukergin, K. G. & Gürlek, M. (2020). "What if this is my last chance?" Developing a last-chance tourism motivation model. *Journal of Destination Marketing & Management*, 18, 100491.

Kvasova, O. (2015). The Big Five personality traits as antecedents of eco-friendly tourist behavior. *Personality and Individual Differences*, 83, 111–116.

Lane, D. (1996). The Gorbachev revolution: The role of the political elite in regime disintegration. *Political Studies*, 44(1), 4–23.

Latour, B. (2004). Whose cosmos, which cosmopolitics? Comments on the peace terms of Ulrich Beck. *Common Knowledge*, 10(3), 450–462.

Layne, C. (2006). The unipolar illusion revisited: The coming end of the United States' unipolar moment. *International Security*, 31(2), 7–41.

Lemelin, H., Dawson, J., Stewart, E. J., Maher, P., & Lueck, M. (2010). Last-chance tourism: The boom, doom, and gloom of visiting vanishing destinations. *Current Issues in Tourism*, 13(5), 477–493.

Lennon, A. T. J. & Kozlowski, A. (2008). *Global Powers in the 21st Century: Strategies and Relations*, Massachusetts: MIT Press (Washington Quarterly Reader).

Lennon, J. & Foley, M. (2000). *Dark Tourism: The Attraction of Death and Disaster*, London: Continuum.

Lenzen, M., Sun, Y. Y., Faturay, F., Ting, Y. P., Geschke, A., & Malik, A. (2018). The carbon footprint of global tourism. *Nature Climate Change*, 8(6), 522–528.

Linklater, A. (2009). The English School. In S. Burchill, A. Linklater, R. Devetak, J. Donelly, T. Nardin, M. Patterson, C. Reus-Smit & J. True (eds), *Theories of International Relations*, 4th ed., London: Palgrave Macmillan, pp. 86–110.

Lodge, T. (2007). *Mandela: A Critical Life*, Oxford University Press: Oxford.

Luh Sin, H., Oakes, T., & Mostafanezhad, M. (2015). Traveling for a cause: Critical examinations of volunteer tourism and social justice. *Tourist Studies*, 15(2), 119–131.

MacCannell, D. (1973). Staged authenticity: Arrangements of social space in tourist settings. *American Journal of Sociology*, 79(3), 589–603.

Mancini, M. S., Evans, M., Iha, K., Danelutti, C., & Galli, A. (2018). Assessing the ecological footprint of ecotourism packages: A methodological proposition. *Resources*, 7(2), 38.

March, J. G. and Olsen, J. P. (2008). The logic of appropriateness. In R. E. Goodin, M. Moran & M. Rein (eds), *The Oxford Handbook of Public Policy*, Oxford University Press, pp. 1–28.

Marzouki, M., Froger, G., & Ballet, J. (2012). Ecotourism versus mass tourism: A comparison of environmental impacts based on ecological footprint analysis. *Sustainability*, 4(1), 123–140.

McConaghy, C. (2012). The Global Peace Index and the structure of peace. In *Cooperation for a Peaceful and Sustainable World Part 1*, Emerald Group Publishing Limited, pp. 1–33.

McCrae, R. R. & Costa Jr, P. T. (1985). Comparison of EPI and psychoticism scales with measures of the five-factor model of personality. *Personality and Individual Differences*, 6(5), 587–597.

McGehee, N. G. (2014). Volunteer tourism: Evolution, issues and futures. *Journal of Sustainable Tourism*, 22(6), 847–854.

McGrath, P. (2022). Social Tourism. In D. Buhalis (ed.), *Encyclopedia of Tourism Management and Marketing* (Vol. 4), Cheltenham, UK and Northampton, MA, USA: Edward Elgar Publishing, pp. 176–178.

Melissen, J. (2013). Public diplomacy. In P. Kerr and G. Wiseman (eds), *Diplomacy in a Globalizing World: Theories and Practices*, Oxford University Press, pp. 192–208.

Mendoza, J. M. & Russo, A. P. (2022). Mobile gentrifiers and leavers: Tourist dwelling as an agent of exclusion in Barcelona. In A. Farmaki, D. Ioannides & S. Kladou (eds), *Peer-to-peer Accommodation and Community Resilience: Implications for Sustainable Development*, CABI, pp. 1–17.

Miller, R. F. (1991). *Soviet Foreign Policy Today: Gorbachev and the New Political Thinking*, Psychology Press.

Mingst, K. A., McKibben, H. E., & Arreguin-Toft, I. M. (2018). *Essentials of International Relations*, WW Norton & Company.

Mishra, J., Mishra, P., & Arora, N. K. (2021). Linkages between environmental issues and zoonotic diseases: with reference to COVID-19 pandemic. *Environmental Sustainability*, 4(3), 455–467.

Molz, J. G. (2006). Cosmopolitan bodies: Fit to travel and travelling to fit. *Body and Society*, 12(3), 1–21.

Moolakkattu, J. S. (2009). Robert W. Cox and critical theory of international relations. *International Studies*, 46(4), 439–456.

Moufakkir, O. & Kelly, I. (eds), (2010). *Tourism, Progress and Peace*, CABI.

Müller, H. (2004). Arguing, bargaining and all that: Communicative action, rationalist theory and the logic of appropriateness in international relations. *European Journal of International Relations*, 10(3): 395–435.

Nardin, T. (2009). International political theory. In S. Burchill, A. Linklater, R. Devetak, J. Donelly, T. Nardin, M. Patterson, C. Reus-Smit & J. True (eds), *Theories of International Relations*, 4th ed., London: Palgrave Macmillan, pp. 284–310.

Neack, L. (2008). *The New Foreign Policy: Power Seeking in a Globalized Era*, Plymouth: Rowman and Littlefield Publishers.

Nedyalkov, N. (May 2019). Why volunteering in Africa might be a bad idea [Video]. *TED Conferences. Why Volunteering in Africa might be a Bad Idea | Nikolay Nedyalkov | TEDxAUBG*.

Neulinger, J. (1984). Key questions evoked by a state of mind conceptualization of leisure. *Loisir et Société/Society and Leisure*, 7(1), 23–36.

Newman, E. (2009). Failed states and international order: Constructing a post-Westphalian world. *Contemporary Security Policy*, 30(3), 421–443.

Nguyen, T. H. H. & Cheung, C. (2016). Chinese heritage tourists to heritage sites: What are the effects of heritage motivation and perceived authenticity on satisfaction? *Asia Pacific Journal of Tourism Research*, 21(11), 1155–1168.

Nisbett, M. (2017). Empowering the empowered? Slum tourism and the depoliticization of poverty. *Geoforum*, 85, 37–45.

Onuf, N. (1995). Levels. *European Journal of International Relations*, 1(1), 35–58.

Pandey, G. (1997). Partition and Independence in Delhi: 1947–48. *Economic and Political Weekly*, 32(36), 2261–2272.

Payne, G. (2009). Trends in global public relations and grassroots diplomacy. *American Behavioral Scientist*, 53(4), 487–492.

Payne, G., Sevin, E., & Bruya, S. (2011). Grassroots 2.0: Public diplomacy in the digital age. *Comunicação Pública*, 6(10), 45–70.

Petras, J. (1994). Cultural imperialism in late 20th century. *Economic and Political Weekly*, 2070–2073.

Phillips, T., Taylor, J., Narain, E., & Chandler, P. (2021). Selling authentic happiness: Indigenous wellbeing and romanticized inequality in tourism advertising. *Annals of Tourism Research*, 87, 103–115.

Pigman, G. A. (2013). Debates about Contemporary and Future Diplomacy. In P. Kerr & G. Wiseman (eds), *Diplomacy in a Globalizing World: Theories and Practices*, Oxford University Press, pp. 68–84.

Piore, M. J. and Sabel, C. F. (1984). *The Second Industrial Divide: Possibilities for Prosperity*, Basic Books.

Plog, S. C. (1974). Why destinations rise and fall in popularity. *Cornell Hotel and Restaurant Administration Quarterly*, 14(4), 55–58.

Plog, S. (2001). Why destination areas rise and fall in popularity: An update of a Cornell Quarterly classic. *Cornell Hotel and Restaurant Administration Quarterly*, 42(3), 13–24.

Podoshen, J. S. (2013). Dark tourism motivations: Simulation, emotional contagion and topographic comparison. *Tourism Management*, 35, 263–271.

Powell, R. (1994). Anarchy in international relations theory: The neorealist–neoliberal debate. *International Organization*, 48(2), 313–344.

Pratt, S. & Liu, A. (2016). Does tourism really lead to peace? A global view. *International Journal of Tourism Research*, 18(1), 82–90.

Rahmani, Z. & Carr, A. (2022). Holistic tourism. In D. Buhalis (ed.), *Encyclopedia of Tourism Management and Marketing* (Vol. 2), Cheltenham, UK and Northampton, MA, USA: Edward Elgar Publishing, pp. 539–541.

Ram, Y., Kama, A., Mizrachi, I., & Hall, C. M. (2019). The benefits of an LGBT-inclusive tourist destination. *Journal of Destination Marketing & Management*, 14, 100374.

Ramsbotham, O. & Woodhouse, T. (1999). *Encyclopedia of International Peacekeeping Operations*, Santa Barbara, CA: ABC-CLIO.

Reality Tours and Travel, 2020. https://realitytoursandtravel.com/dharavi-slum-tours/. Accessed on 27 December, 2021.

Rettman, A. (2022). Paris and Berlin pledge Russia sanctions, but not visa ban. *EUObserver*. https://euobserver.com/world/155915. Accessed on 2 September 2022.

Reus-Smit, C. (2009). Constructivism. In S. Burchill, A. Linklater, R. Devetak, J. Donelly, T. Nardin, M. Patterson, C. Reus-Smit & J. True (eds), *Theories of International Relations*, 4th ed., London: Palgrave Macmillan, pp. 212–236.

Richmond, O. P. & Mitchell, A. (2011). *Hybrid Forms of Peace: From Everyday Agency to Post-liberalism*, Springer.

Risse, T. (2000). Let's argue! Communicative action in world politics. *International Organization*, 54(01), 1–39.

Risse, T. (2007). Transnational actors and world politics. In W. C. Zimmerli, M. Holzinger & K. Richter (eds), *Corporate Ethics and Corporate Governance*, Berlin Heidelberg: Springer, pp. 251–286.

Ritzer, G. (1992). *The McDonaldization of Society*, Sage Publications.

Robert, K. W., Parris, T. M., & Leiserowitz, A. A. (2005). What is sustainable development? Goals, indicators, values, and practice. *Environment: Science and Policy for Sustainable Development*, 47(3), 8–21.

Rosenberg, T. (2018). The business of voluntourism: Do western do-gooders actually do harm? *The Guardian*, 13 September 2018.

Rourke, J. T. & Boyer, M. A. (2008). *International Politics on the World Stage*, New York: McGraw-Hill.

Ruhanen, L. & Axelsen, M. (2022). Ecotourism. In D. Buhalis (ed.), *Encyclopedia of Tourism Management and Marketing* (Vol. 2), Cheltenham, UK and Northampton, MA, USA: Edward Elgar Publishing, pp. 27–31.

Scheyvens, R. & Biddulph, R. (2018). Inclusive tourism development. *Tourism Geographies*, 20(4), 589–609.

SCORE (2015). *Predicting Peace: The Social Cohesion and Reconciliation Index as a Tool for Conflict Transformation*, Cyprus: UNDP-Action for Cooperation and Trust.

SCORE (2022). *The Social Cohesion and Reconciliation Index (SCORE)*. https://www.scoreforpeace.org/en. Accessed on 3 September 2022.

Seaton, A. V. (1996). Guided by the dark: From thanatopsis to thanatourism. *International Journal of Heritage Studies*, 2(4), 234–244.

Servas International (2022). www.servas.org, Accessed on 20 June 2022.

Shakibi, Z. (2010). *Khatami and Gorbachev: Politics of Change in the Islamic Republic of Iran and the USSR*, IB Tauris.

Sharpley, R. (2000). Tourism and sustainable development: Exploring the theoretical divide. *Journal of Sustainable Tourism*, 8(1), 1–19.

Sharpley, R. (2020). Tourism, sustainable development and the theoretical divide: 20 years on. *Journal of Sustainable Tourism*, 28(11), 1932–1946.

Sharpley, R. (2021). On the need for sustainable tourism consumption. *Tourist Studies*, 21(1), 96–107.

Sharpley, R. & Stone. P. (2009). *The Darker Side of Travel: Theory and Practice of Dark Tourism*. Bristol: Channel View.

Sharpley, R. & Ussi, M. (2014). Tourism and governance in small island developing states (SIDS): The case of Zanzibar. *International Journal of Tourism Research*, 16(1), 87–96.

Skidmore, J. (2008). Britons: More mean than green. *Daily Telegraph: Telegraph Travel*, 14 June, T4.

Smith, K. E. I. (2018). What is globalization? In K. E. I. Smith (ed.), *Sociology of Globalization*, Routledge, pp. 3–10.

Snellings, S. (2019). The "gayification" of Tel Aviv: Examining Israel's pro-gay brand. *Queer Cats*, 3–4.

Solomon, A. (2015). Authenticity and simulation in post-tourism. *Synergy*, 11(1), 41–53.

Spies, Y. K. (2019). Polylateral diplomacy: Diplomacy as public–private collaboration. In Y. K. Spies, *Global South Perspectives on Diplomacy*, Palgrave Macmillan, Cham, pp. 153–199.

Stone, P. (2005). Consuming dark tourism: A call for research. *Review of Tourism Research*, 3(5).

Stone, P. (2006). A dark tourism spectrum: Towards a typology of death and macabre related tourist sites, attractions and exhibitions. *Tourism: An Interdisciplinary International Journal*, 54(2), 145–160.

Stone, P. & Sharpley, R. (2008). Consuming dark tourism: A thanatological perspective. *Annals of Tourism Research*, 35(2), 574–595.

Stone, P. & Sharpley, R. (2013). Deviance, dark tourism and "dark leisure": Towards a (re) configuration of morality and the taboo in secular society. In S. Elkington & S. J. Gammon (eds), *Contemporary Perspectives in Leisure*, Routledge, pp. 76–86.

Stors, N. & Kagermeier, A. (2013). Crossing the border of the tourist bubble: Touristification in Copenhagen. *Tourismus und Grenzen*, 9, 115–131.

Sun, Y. Y. (2014). A framework to account for the tourism carbon footprint at island destinations. *Tourism Management*, 45, 16–27.

Sutter, R. G. (2012). China's growing international role. In N. Tzifakis (ed.), *International Politics in Times of Change*, Berlin, Heidelberg: Springer, pp. 117–134.

Swain, M. B. (2009). The cosmopolitan hope of tourism: Critical action and worldmaking vistas. *Tourism Geographies*, 11(4), 505–525.

Telfer, D. J. (2002). The evolution of tourism and development theory. In R. Sharpley & D. J. Telfer (eds), *Tourism and Development: Concepts and Issues*, Aspects of Tourism Series, Channel View Publications, pp. 35–80.

Todaro, M. P. & Smith, S. C. (2009). *Economic Development*, Boston: Pearson.

Trauer, B. (2006). Conceptualizing special interest tourism: Frameworks for analysis. *Tourism Management*, 27(2), 183–200.

Turner, B. (2022). Here's what Russia's favourite travel vloggers think of the EU's new visa rules. *Euronews.* https://www.euronews.com/2022/09/02/heres-what -russias-favourite-travel-vloggers-think-of-the-eus-new-visa-rules. Accessed on 2 September 2022.

Tyler, M. C. & Beyerinck, C. (2016). Citizen diplomacy. In C. Constantinou, P. Kerr, & P. Sharp (Eds.), *The SAGE Handbook of Diplomacy*, pp. 521–529.

UNDP (2015). Final Report: Action for Cooperation and Trust in Cyprus, 1 October 2005–31 December 2015, *United Nations Development Programme*.

UNDP (2022). About us. *United Nations Development Programme.* https://www.undp .org/about-us/. Accessed on 25 August 2022.

UNDP Libya (2022). Libya: UNDP and national partners deepen collaboration with new Country Programme focused on sustainable growth and peacebuilding. *United Nations Development Programme.* https://www.undp.org/libya/press-releases/undp -and-national-partners-deepen-collaboration-new-country-programme-focused-sust ainable-growth-and-peacebuilding. Accessed on 25 August 2022.

UNDP-ACT (2008). Building Lasting Relationships Islandwide. *Action for Cooperation and Trust in Cyprus*.

United Nations (2022). *The 17 Goals.* Department of Economic and Social Affairs, United Nations. https://sdgs.un.org/goals. Accessed on 8 March 2022.

United Nations (2022a). Principles of peacekeeping. https://peacekeeping.un.org/en/ principles-of-peacekeeping Accessed on 14 June 2022.

Urry, J. (1990). *The Tourist Gaze: Leisure and Travel in Contemporary Societies,* London: Sage Publications.

Urry, J. (1996). Tourism, culture, and social inequality. In Y. Apostolopoulos, S. Leivadi & A. Yiannakis (eds), *The Sociology of Tourism: Theoretical and Empirical Investigations,* Routledge, pp. 115–133.

Urry, J. (2002). *Consuming Places,* Chicago: Routledge.

Usai, R., Cai, W., & Wassler, P. (2022). A queer perspective on heteronormativity for LGBT travelers. *Journal of Travel Research,* 61(1), 3–15.

Valtonen, A., Rantala, O., Salmela, T., & Höckert, E. (2020). Envisioning tourism and proximity after the anthropocene. *Sustainability,* 12(10), 3948.

Vaxevanidou, M. (2017). Nation rebranding in a period of crisis and the role of public diplomacy: The case study of Greece. *Journal of Media Critiques,* 3(11), 57–71.

Verma, V. K., Kumar, S., & Chandra, B. (2017). Big Five personality traits and tourist's intention to visit green hotels. *Indian Journal of Scientific Research,* 15(2), 79–87.

Vision of Humanity. (2022). *RESOURCES: IEP's Peace Research, Presentations and Resources.* www.visionofhumanity.org. Accessed on 25 August 2022.

Waller, J. & Lea, S. E. (1999). Seeking the real Spain? Authenticity in motivation. *Annals of Tourism Research,* 26(1), 110–129.

Waltz, K. (2004). Neorealism: Confusions and criticisms. *Journal of Politics and Society,* 15(1), 2–6.

Welt, C. (2010). The thawing of a frozen conflict: The internal security dilemma and the 2004 prelude to the Russo–Georgian War. *Europe–Asia Studies,* 62(1), 63–97.

Wendt, A. E. (1987). The agent–structure problem in international relations theory. *International Organization,* 41(03), 335–370.

Wendt, A. E. (1992). Anarchy is what states make of it: The social construction of power politics. *International Organization,* 46(02), 391–425.

Wernick, D. A. & Von Glinow, M. A. (2012). Reflections on the evolving terrorist threat to luxury hotels: A case study on Marriott International. *Thunderbird International Business Review,* 54(5), 729–746.

Wight, M. (1977). *Systems of States,* Leicester University Press.

Wiseman, G. & Basu, S. (2013). The United Nations. In P. Kerr & G. Wiseman (eds), *Diplomacy in a Globalizing World: Theories and Practices,* Oxford University Press, pp. 319–335.

Wohlforth, W. C. (1999). The stability of a unipolar world. *International Security,* 24(1), 5–41.

Woolcock, S. (2013). Economic diplomacy. In P. Kerr & G. Wiseman (eds), *Diplomacy in a Globalizing World: Theories and Practices,* Oxford University Press.

Yang, E. C. L. & Nair, V. (2014). Tourism at risk: A review of risk and perceived risk in tourism. *Asia-Pacific Journal of Innovation in Hospitality and Tourism,* 3(2), 239–259.

Zartman, I. W. (Ed.). (2007). *Peacemaking in international conflict: Methods & Techniques,* US Institute of Peace Press.

Zartman, I. W. (2013). Diplomacy as negotiation and mediation. In P. Kerr & G. Wiseman (eds), *Diplomacy in a Globalizing World: Theories and Practices,* Oxford University Press, pp. 103–120.

Index